Maxim Gorky

Twayne's World Authors Series
Russian Literature

Charles Moser, Editor

TWAS 781

MAXIM GORKY, 1903
Photograph by K. A. Fisher.

Maxim Gorky

By Barry P. Scherr

Dartmouth College

Twayne Publishers
A Division of G. K. Hall & Co. • *Boston*

Maxim Gorky

Barry P. Scherr

Copyright 1988 by G. K. Hall & Co.
All rights reserved.
Published by Twayne Publishers
A Division of G. K. Hall & Co.
70 Lincoln Street
Boston, Massachusetts 02111

Copyediting supervised by Lewis DeSimone
Book production by Janet Zietowski
Book design by Barbara Anderson

Typeset in 11 pt. Garamond
by Modern Graphics, Inc., Weymouth, Massachusetts

Printed on permanent/durable acid-free paper
and bound in the United States of America

Library of Congress Cataloging in Publication Data
Scherr, Barry P.
    Maxim Gorky/by Barry P. Scherr.
        p. cm.—(Twayne's world authors series ; TWAS 781. Russian literature)
    Bibliography: p.
    Includes index.
    ISBN 0-8057-6636-7 (alk. paper)
    1. Gorky, Maksim, 1868–1936. 2. Authors, Russian—20th century—
Biography. I. Title. II. Series: Twayne's world authors series ; TWAS
781. III. Series: Twayne's world authors series. Russian literature.
PG3465.S34 1988
891.78'309—dc19
[B]   87–17202

To Sylvia

Contents

About the Author

Barry Scherr is professor of Russian at Dartmouth College. He received his B.A. from Harvard College and his M.A. and Ph.D. from the University of Chicago. Before coming to Dartmouth in 1974, he taught at the University of Washington in Seattle. His special interests include Russian prose of the first third of the twentieth century, Russian verse theory, and computer-assisted language instruction in Russian. His articles on these topics have appeared in various scholarly journals, and he is the author of the book *Russian Poetry: Meter, Rhythm, and Rhyme.*

Preface

Maxim Gorky was an extremely prominent figure in Russian literature from the 1890s until his death in 1936. He achieved renown for his writing in several genres: first the short story, then the novel, drama, autobiography, and memoirs. Nor was his significance limited to his creative writing. A prolific essayist, he devoted numerous articles to literature as well as to social and political issues. Soon after Gorky became an established author he emerged as the acknowledged leader among the so-called "critical realists," a loosely knit group of writers who adhered to the realistic manner among the great novelists of the nineteenth century and who also criticized many aspects of their contemporary society. He began his extensive editing and publishing pursuits with the establishment of the *Znanie* [Knowledge] anthologies, which published many of the critical realists' works. Gorky was also a political activist all his adult life, and was persecuted on more than one occasion for his support of revolutionary movements. While his relationship with Lenin and other Bolshevik leaders was not always smooth, his early allegiance to their cause gave him a degree of authority when they took power. Gorky did all he could to provide both material relief and publishing opportunities for writers in the difficult years immediately following the October Revolution; his assistance was crucial in helping many writers survive. Deeply involved in both political and literary affairs in Russia during one of the most turbulent periods in its history, acquainted with many of the leading personalities of his day, and living an eventful life both in Russia and abroad, Gorky was a writer whose biography, which still awaits adequate treatment, is every bit as important as his works.

Over the years Gorky's reputation has fared quite differently at home and abroad. Within the Soviet Union he enjoys the status of a highly respected classic, the "father of Soviet literature." He is widely studied in schools and universities, and hardly a year passes without the publication of at least one book—to say nothing of dozens of articles—devoted to his writing. In the West Gorky was quite famous during his lifetime, when many of his works came out in translation almost simultaneously with their appearance in

Russian. Today, though, his reputation is more modest. Despite a recent revival, the critics have paid him only sporadic attention. Most English-speaking readers know his work only through a sampling of his plays, most notably *The Lower Depths (Na dne)*, his one work that continues to command an international audience. Others may have read his autobiographical writings, a few short stories, or one of his novels. Few, even among students of Russian literature, are familiar with the bulk of his writing.

A major goal of this study is to acquaint Western readers with a wide range of Gorky's oeuvre, and in so doing to suggest that certain works have been unjustly neglected. In particular, I make an effort to demonstrate that the manner of writing that worked so successfully for Gorky in such disparate items as *The Lower Depths* and his autobiographical trilogy can be found—and was perfected— in writings that have received much less acclaim. Since Gorky's output was vast—his fiction alone occupies some twenty-five volumes in the most recent complete edition—individual pieces are grouped both by genre and by chronology. The literary analysis begins in Chapter 2 with the stories, the chief genre in which he worked during the initial stage of his career. The following chapters discuss his prerevolutionary novels, which were, except for one immature work, all composed between 1899 and 1911, and the prerevolutionary plays, which began to appear in 1902. Chapter 5 surveys Gorky's autobiographical writings and literary memoirs, genres in which he worked intensively during the 1910s and on into the 1920s. Gorky's postrevolutionary stories, plays, and novels are then examined together in Chapter 6. I have been selective in discussing Gorky's numerous stories, and his essays on literature and journalism for the most part remain beyond the scope of this study.

The dates for Gorky's works indicate the year of completion; in cases when the writing took several years, or seems to have been equally divided between two years, inclusive dates are provided. Translations from the Russian are my own. I use the Library of Congress system without diacritics for transliterating Russian names and titles; however, in the main body of the text commonly accepted versions of proper names are employed instead—hence Gor'kii in the title of a work in the notes, but Gorky in the text.

I am grateful to the National Endowment for the Humanities, which awarded me a summer stipend to permit a period of concentrated work on this study. My thanks go to Patricia Carter of Dartmouth's Interlibrary Loan Office, who with good cheer obtained many items that I needed, often on short notice. I am also indebted to Nellie Plummer, who assisted in preparing the manuscript. Over the years I have benefited greatly from the insights and suggestions of Richard Sheldon and Lev Loseff, on this project as well as on others, and I express my appreciation to both. Finally, I dedicate this book to my wife for her help, her support, and, at so many moments, encouragement.

Barry P. Scherr

Dartmouth College

Chronology

1868	Alexei Maximovich Peshkov born 16 March in Nizhny Novgorod (now Gorky), a major trade and manufacturing center on the Volga.
1871	Family moves to Astrakhan. Father dies of cholera. Alexei and mother return to Nizhny Novgorod.
1879	His mother dies of consumption. Alexei apprenticed to work in shoe store.
1880–1884	Apprenticed to V. S. Sergeev, a building contractor. At intervals leaves this position for other work, serving in a workshop of icon painters and on boats.
1884–1888	In Kazan. Works in various bakeshops, becomes involved with radical groups.
1887	Death of his grandmother (February) and of his grandfather (May). Attempts suicide 12 December.
1888	Spends summer with Mikhail Romas, a revolutionary activist, in a village near Kazan.
1889	Returns to Nizhny Novgorod; begins to work for a lawyer.
1891	Leaves Nizhny Novgorod and begins long journey on foot through Russia, wandering through the Ukraine, the Crimea, and the Caucasus.
1892	Travels about Georgia. The Tiflis newspaper *Kavkaz* [Caucasus] publishes his first story, "Makar Chudra," 12 September, signed "M. Gorky."
1895	Gorky's stories continue to appear regularly in Volga newspapers. "Chelkash" appears in a leading Moscow journal.
1896	Marries Ekaterina Pavlovna Volzhina.
1897	Birth of his son Maxim 27 July.
1898	Two-volume edition of his short stories published in Saint Petersburg. Beginning of great popular acclaim.

In May arrested and imprisoned for two weeks in Tiflis because of his connection with Social Democrats.

1899 Novel *Foma Gordeev* published. Makes first visit to Saint Petersburg and becomes literary editor of the Marxist journal *Zhizn'* [Life].

1900 Meets Tolstoy for the first time in Moscow.

1901 Arrested and imprisoned for a month in Nizhny Novgorod for revolutionary activities. Birth of daughter Ekaterina, 26 May.

1902 Production of Gorky's first two plays, *The Petty Bourgeois (Meshchane)* and *The Lower Depths (Na dne)*. Elected honorary member of Academy of Sciences. When the tsar annuls the election Chekhov and Korolenko resign in protest. Summer: forced to reside in Arzamas.

1905 Witnesses events of "Bloody Sunday," 9 January. Arrested after composing protest letter; later released on bail. Joins Bolshevik party; meets Lenin.

1906 Trip to America to organize support and raise money for the Bolshevik cause. Travels with the actress Maria Andreeva, which results in scandal in New York. In the United States writes novel *Mother (Mat')* and play *Enemies (Vragi)*. His daugter dies in Russia 16 August. Gorky and Andreeva go to Capri, where Gorky stays until 1913.

1908 *A Confession (Ispoved')*. Interest in "God-building." Lenin visits Gorky on Capri.

1910 Begins publication of *The Life of Matvei Kozhemiakin (Zhizn' Matveia Kozhemiakina)*.

1913 Begins publication of *Childhood (Detstvo)*. Returns to Russia under amnesty granted to mark the three hundredth anniversary of the Romanov dynasty.

1915 Organizes a new journal, *Letopis'* [The Chronicle].

1916 *In the World (V liudiakh)* published.

1917 Helps found newspaper *Novaya zhizn'* [New Life]. Starts publishing his "Untimely Thoughts" as a regular column.

1918   *Novaya zhizn'* closed. Begins organizing the World Literature publishing house.

1919–1921   Aids writers and others involved in cultural pursuits. In 1921 leaves Russia for medical treatment.

1923   Helps establish journal *Beseda* [Dialogue] in Berlin. *My Universities (Moi universitety)* appears.

1924   Goes to Italy for a cure; settles in Sorrento.

1925   *The Artamonovs (Delo Artamonovykh)* is published in Berlin. Begins work on *The Life of Klim Samgin (Zhizn' Klima Samgina)*, which remains unfinished at the time of his death.

1928   Arrives for a triumphant visit to the Soviet Union 27 May. Thereafter makes several long visits to the Soviet Union before settling there permanently in 1933.

1932   Publication of *Egor Bulychov and Others (Egor Bulychov i drugie)*.

1934   Gorky's son dies 11 May. Delivers opening address at the First All-Union Congress of Soviet Writers and is elected chairman of the Congress.

1936   Dies 18 June.

Chapter One
Writer and Revolutionary
Childhood and Youth

While Maxim Gorky was a prolific and an important writer, his biography equals and perhaps even surpasses his literary work in lasting significance. From the adventure-filled wanderings of his youth, through his acquaintance with leading literary and political figures of his time, to his active work on behalf of the revolutionary cause and of his fellow authors, there is hardly a year in Gorky's mature life that does not reward intense study. Indeed, his experiences are important not just for their own sake, but also because they are reflected in so many of his works—not only his autobiographical writings and memoirs, but also most of his fiction is dependent on direct observation.

While much has been written about Gorky's life, we still lack a complete biography. Thus many aspects of his career await full elucidation: the reasons for his meteoric rise to leadership among his fellow writers; his attitudes toward Bolshevism when he was living abroad during the 1920s; his activities in the Soviet Union after he returned there permanently; even the cause of his death. In a brief chapter we can do no more than provide an outline of the more important events in his life and offer suggestions about matters that remain obscure.

Alexei Maximovich Peshkov was born on 16 March 1868, in the town of Nizhny Novgorod, a major trade and manufacturing center on the Volga river since renamed Gorky in his honor.[1] He took the nom de plume "M. Gorky" (Gorky is the Russian word for bitter) only in 1892, when he published his first story, "Makar Chudra."[2] Maxim Peshkov, Gorky's father, was a carpenter and a cabinet-maker; his mother, Varvara, was the daughter of the owner of a small dye-works. When Alexei was barely three, Maxim Peshkov took his family to Astrakhan, a town further south on the Volga. That summer a cholera epidemic swept through the community. Alexei fell ill but recovered; his father, however, possibly infected

1

by his own son, died of cholera in July 1871. Varvara took Alexei back to Nizhny Novgorod and went to live with her parents, Vasily and Akulina Kashirin.

The death of his father and the subsequent move to his grandparents' home had important consequences for Alexei. Both his grandfather and grandmother became dominant figures of his childhood. Akulina Kashirina told Alexei numerous fairy tales and instilled in him a love for folklore that influenced his writing all his life. At the same time her passivity when faced with the cruelty and violence surrounding her was an attitude he ultimately rejected. His grandfather had worked hard to establish his dye-works and had been an elder in the town.[3] Although Vasily's fortunes declined precipitously during his grandson's childhood, he provided Alexei with his first example of the successful entrepreneur who figures in much of his writing. For that matter, the entire Kashirin family—the patriarchal grandfather, the dissolute second generation, and the "lost" third generation—offered a model that served Gorky well.[4]

Second, without a father the boy was left more to his own devices than he might have been otherwise, and so he grew up an independent soul. Third, he was firmly ensconced in a lower middle-class existence that provided an angle from which to view the world about him. By nineteenth-century standards his upbringing, while certainly not luxurious, was not totally impoverished. Even after his grandfather's fortunes declined the boy was apprenticed to a fairly well-off relative, and he did receive an elementary education. Alexei's experience was not that of a proletarian somehow "born" to be a revolutionary, nor was he an intellectual attracted to abstract political ideas. He came from the class of people who were as likely to become reactionaries as revolutionaries.[5] In fact, his final, uncompleted novel, the four-volume *Life of Klim Samgin,* traced the career of a person of similar background whose life developed in an opposite direction from Gorky's own.

Nevertheless, Alexei's early years were by no means easy. The Kashirin family was quarrelsome and oftentimes violent. His mother displayed only sporadic interest in him and in 1876 married a student, Evgeny Maximov, who was somewhat younger than she and turned out to be a ne'er-do-well.[6] The first part of Gorky's autobiographical trilogy, *Childhood,* ends with the death of his mother in 1879, when she was not yet thirty-five and Alexei only eleven.

After that he entered upon a series of apprenticeships, working in a shoe store, in a workshop where icons were painted, and, at various intervals, for his cousin Vasily Sergeev, a building contractor. On a couple of occasions he was a helper on ships that sailed the Volga. During this period Alexei became familiar with the classics of Russian literature—Pushkin, Lermontov—and also read translations of foreign novels. He had a special fondness for French literature and devoured the works of Balzac, Stendhal, and Flaubert.[7] The love of reading, and of learning in general, stayed with him all his life; a new work, if of any worth at all, could easily move him to tears.[8] His extraordinary efforts to encourage beginning writers may be explained in part by this youthful infatuation with literature.

In 1884 Alexei left Nizhny Novgorod for Kazan, yet another Volga city, where he hoped to enter the university, but his haphazard education and lack of financial support soon put an end to his dream. He returned to doing odd jobs. For some months he toiled fourteen hours a day in a bakery, an experience that provided him with the material for several of his best stories. From that bakery he went to another, run by Andrei Derenkov, a shopowner involved with radical political movements who used his profits to support progressive causes. Alexei's connection to the Derenkov family, which dated back to the early months of his stay in Kazan, gave him the opportunity to read books by radical thinkers from the Derenkovs' secret library and also to meet various activists in Kazan. Thus this period marked the beginning of Gorky's political concerns, though his involvement with any one circle was never total. Even later, when he became an active supporter of the Bolsheviks, he was more an ardent revolutionary than a loyal adherent of the party line.[9] Alexei's ingrained independence later caused difficulties in his relationships with Lenin and other Bolshevik leaders.

Early in 1887 Alexei's grandmother died, to be followed a few months later by his grandfather. Their deaths do not appear to have affected him greatly, for by then he had left his childhood far behind, but the swirl of impressions arising from his experiences and his readings led to a crisis. Exhausted by work, still disappointed by his failure to obtain a higher education, and unsure of what to do with his life, he decided to shoot himself. On 12 December he fired a bullet into his left side but missed his heart. After a little over a week in the hospital he returned to work in Derenkov's bakery.

While the shock of his suicide attempt apparently ended his

immediate depression, Gorky soon decided to leave Kazan and try
something new. In June of 1888 Mikhail Romas, a revolutionary
activist, invited Alexei to work with him among the peasants in
Krasnovidovo, a small village near Kazan. Their propaganda efforts
ended when the shop that Romas had established was burned down
and Romas fled. Gorky left with another of the propagandists in
what proved the beginning of his years of wandering. Although
during the next several years Gorky spent much time back in Nizhny
Novgorod, he also tramped through a good part of Russia, gathering
the impressions that were to serve as the basis for many of his future
writings.

The Young Writer

Our knowledge of Gorky's next few years is based partly on his
published writings, partly on his letters, and to a degree on memoirs
by eyewitnesses, though the latter are not always totally accurate
or complete.[10] Still, the rough outlines of Gorky's activities can be
discerned. He spent the fall season of 1888 working at a fishery on
the shore of the Caspian Sea, after which he found employment in
several places as a railway watchman. Then, along with several other
people in a discussion group, he conceived the notion of establishing
an agrarian, self-sufficient community. He set out to find the most
prominent advocate of such a life, Lev Tolstoy, wishing to ask him
for a piece of land on which his group could realize its ambition;
but when he could not locate Tolstoy either at his estate or at his
Moscow home, Gorky returned to Nizhny Novgorod in the spring
of 1889.[11]

Gorky spent almost two years in his hometown working in the
law offices of A. I. Lanin. During this time he met the writer
Vladimir Korolenko, who was then living there and who read Gorky's first literary efforts.[12] In 1891 Gorky set out to wander through
southern Russia. He tramped along the Volga and Don rivers, visited
the Ukraine and the Crimea, and ended up in the Caucasus, living
for a while in Tiflis (now Tbilisi), where he published "Makar
Chudra" in the newspaper *Kavkaz* [Caucasus]. Late in 1892 he
returned to Nizhny Novgorod, went back to work for Lanin, and
entered into a common-law marriage with Olga Kaminskaya, an
artist and political activist.[13] By this time Gorky was a budding
young writer, and his stories began to appear in various regional
newspapers.[14]

Gorky's career developed quickly. Thanks to Korolenko's patronage, the story "Chelkash" appeared in the June 1895 issue of *Russkoe bogatstvo* [Russian Wealth], a prominent Moscow journal. By then Gorky had already parted with Olga Kaminskaya and moved to Samara, where he worked as a feature writer on the local paper: as a result of some unexpected departures, Gorky soon found himself its editor.[15] Thus professional newspaper work was for several years a major activity, along with his fiction. In 1896 he came back to Nizhny Novgorod, where he joined the staff of *Nizhegorodskii listok* [Nizhny Novgorod News], in its prime one of the best provincial newspapers in Russia.[16] Simultaneously he worked as a correspondent for an Odessa paper and thus was busy writing one story after another. His literary reputation was already beginning to spread.

Meanwhile there were changes in his personal life. In Samara he fell in love with Ekaterina Pavlovna Volzhina, his paper's proofreader, and they married in 1896. The following year their son Maxim was born, and in 1901 a daughter Ekaterina. The marriage did not last long; the two were already beginning to drift apart before their daughter's birth, and by the end of 1903 Maria Andreeva, an actress with the Moscow Art Theater, had become Gorky's common-law wife. Nevertheless, Gorky and Ekaterina Pavlovna remained on friendly terms for the rest of his life, and after his death she helped gather and publish materials relating to his life and work.

Gorky's fame as a writer dates from 1898, when his *Sketches and Stories (Ocherki i rasskazy)* appeared in two volumes. Other writers have also gained renown overnight, but Gorky's case may be unique. As Alexander Kaun writes: "Everywhere one could see his picture— on postal cards, cigarette- and candy-boxes, and in endless cartoons. Shady characters stopped citizens in the street and asked for, or rather demanded, 'a bottle of vodka in the name of Maxim Gorky.' . . . In various cities there even appeared pseudo-Gorkys, who posed as the original and tried to make use of his popularity. Gorky's costume—a Russian blouse and high boots, became the vogue, and even society ladies considered it fashionable to lisp French phrases concerning those charming *bosyaks* [vagabonds]."[17]

These last two points hint at the reasons for Gorky's popularity. First, his subject matter—Russia's outcasts and tramps—captured people's romantic fancy. Second, Gorky himself was not beyond cultivating an image. His studiously rustic dress set him apart from the conventional city writer and was as easily recognizable as the subject matter of his stories. Perhaps the themes of his works, his unusual biography, and his political activities would have brought him a reputation in any case, but Gorky himself did much to promote his fame.

Almost from the moment his *Sketches and Stories* were published, Gorky moved rapidly into literary society. He met Chekhov (with whom he entered into an intense correspondence) and Tolstoy; about both he later wrote brilliant memoirs (see Chap. 5). Their mutual acquaintance was nurtured during frequent sojourns in the Crimea, where all three writers spent time for reasons of health. Chekhov by then was already seriously ill with the tuberculosis that was to kill him in 1904. Gorky had also been diagnosed as having tuberculosis in 1896, and while he eventually largely recovered, his health was poor for the rest of his life.

Among younger writers Gorky was closest to those Russian critics often labeled the "critical realists." They tended to write about both the malaise of the intelligentsia and about Russia's lower classes; several of them had gathered in the *Sreda* [Wednesday] circle, founded by Nikolai Teleshov.[18] Its members included Ivan Bunin, Leonid Andreev, Alexander Kuprin, Evgeny Chirikov, and Skitalets (Stepan Petrov). Gorky quickly became the unofficial leader of the group, urging the members to write socially committed literature, demanding that they be productive, and even taking an interest in their personal life if he felt it was affecting their writing. Gorky began his publishing enterprises while with this group. He had been literary editor of the Marxist journal *Zhizn'* [Life], closed by the authorities in 1901 after it printed Gorky's "Song of the Stormy Petrel" ("Pesnia o Burevestnike"), with its not particularly subtle revolutionary overtones. In 1900 he joined with the collective publishing enterprise *Znanie* [Knowledge]. Founded two years before, at the start it had issued popular scientific publications in mass editions. By 1902 two of those in the original collective—Gorky and K. P. Pyatnitsky—had become its sole members. They began publishing editions of works by the *Sreda* group in press runs that were enormous for the day. Gorky's own writings were constant best-sellers, but works by other members of the group also sold extremely well. In 1904 the first *Znanie* anthologies appeared, and these publications, containing works by *Sreda* writers and some others, also achieved both popular and critical success.[19] After the

1905 revolution and Gorky's subsequent departure from Russia, however, the quality of the publications declined, even though Gorky continued to take an interest in them. The seriousness of Gorky's commitment to *Znanie* and to its literary standards did not always lead to smooth relations between him and his fellow writers. For instance, he wrote to Pyatnitsky from Capri in 1908 criticizing him for publishing a story by Kuprin, who then was still at the height of his fame. Gorky felt that Pyatnitsky had published the work only because it was by a well-known writer.[20] Gorky could criticize others' personal failings, too, as when he wrote a 1903 letter to Pyatnitsky about Andreev's scandalous behavior.[21] Yet his frequent expressions of annoyance—made both directly and through third parties—were inspired by a genuine concern for others: in the same letter in which he condemns Andreev's behavior he worries over Chirikov. Writing to Andreev, he advises him about both his literary endeavors (telling him not to write so rapidly) and about his personal qualities (warning him not to be too anxious for praise).[22]

Gorky's connections with the careers of individual writers could thus be very close.[23] A case in point is Skitalets, whom Gorky had gotten to know in Nizhny Novgorod.[24] Skitalets had already launched his literary career when the two met, and their connection was also partly political. Gorky published a story by Skitalets in *Zhizn'*, thereby introducing him to the leading literary circles. Skitalets became a regular contributor to the *Znanie* anthologies, but Gorky eventually realized that Skitalets was in many ways a limited author, which he had not noticed in his initial enthusiasm for him.[25] A completely different relationship developed between Gorky and Ivan Bunin, who as an émigré became the first Russian author to receive the Nobel Prize for literature. The aristocratic Bunin was much less prone than other young authors to fall under Gorky's sway, and there was always some distance between the two. But from its first issue Bunin was one of the most loyal contributors to the *Znanie* series;[26] later he visited Gorky on Capri and spent a couple of winter seasons living nearby.[27] The revolution drove the two apart: Gorky, even while living abroad during the 1920s, was always hopeful that the Bolshevik government would meet his expectations, while Bunin was bitterly opposed to the new order. Gorky's admiration for fine literature, however, could outweigh his personal feelings, and at least one eyewitness account recalls him as deeply moved by a new story of Bunin's even after they had broken off their personal relations.[28]

Gorky's activities from 1898 on were not solely literary. He maintained close ties to radical circles in both the Nizhny Novgorod area and Moscow. Through his association with *Zhizn'* he was linked to the Marxists in both the literary and the political spheres, and by 1903 he was especially close to the Bolsheviks. But his literary reputation did not shield him from difficulties with the authorities. In 1898, the year his fame began, he was arrested because of his connections with a social-democratic organization in Tiflis and spent sixteen days in prison there. In April 1901 he and Skitalets were arrested for their propaganda work among workers in Sormovo, a district of Nizhny Novgorod (and, the following year, locale of the strike that served as the inspiration for Gorky's novel *Mother*). On this occasion Gorky spent about a month in prison. In 1902 he was forced to live in Arzamas for several months during an investigation of his political activities. When the same year he was elected an honorary member of the Academy of Sciences, the tsar annulled the decision because of Gorky's revolutionary sympathies. In response two of its more prominent honorary members—Korolenko and Chekhov—resigned their memberships.

Despite his deep involvement with politics and his duties as editor and publisher, Gorky still found time to write prolifically. He continued to compose a steady stream of stories, while his first novel, *Foma Gordeev*, appeared in 1899 and his second, *The Three of Them (Troe)*, in 1901. The year 1902 witnessed the appearance of his first two plays, *The Petty Bourgeois* and *The Lower Depths*—the latter, of course, perhaps the single work for which he is best known today. By this time his reputation was no longer national but international. Every year his works were translated into numerous foreign languages; his first two novels, for instance, appeared in English just two years after they were published in Russian. Editions of his work came out regularly throughout Europe and in the United States.[29]

From Revolution to Revolution

By the beginning of 1905 Gorky's life appeared set on its future path. Perhaps the most highly acclaimed writer of his day in Russia, he was deeply involved in various literary enterprises and was a prominent political activist. Events of that year, however, unexpectedly led to Gorky's departure from the country for eight years. On "Bloody Sunday," 9 January, Gorky was in Petersburg when troops fired on a crowd that had come to the Winter Palace to petition Nicholas II for redress of grievances. The event marked the start of year-long disturbances that led to the granting of a constitution and the establishment of the duma, a form of parliament with limited legislative authority. As a witness to Bloody Sunday, Gorky immediately wrote an appeal for struggle against the autocracy and took part in various meetings in which governmental repression was condemned.

The next day the order was issued for Gorky's arrest and on 11 January he was taken in Riga, where he had gone to see the ill Maria Andreeva. During the month he spent in the Peter and Paul Fortress he wrote a play, *Children of the Sun (Deti solntsa)*, which, although set in provincial Russia with no overt political references, contains scenes that recreate the tense atmosphere of the time: when the play premiered in October of that year, the audience nearly panicked at the shooting of a character.[30] After being freed on bail, Gorky maintained contact with the Social Democrats, and in November he met Lenin for the first time. He was in Moscow during the December uprising there and helped build barricades. Since by then he was once again in danger of being arrested, in January of 1906 he went to Finland, and from there to Germany.

For the last two years Gorky had been living with Maria Andreeva, whom he had first met in 1900 when Stanislavsky's Moscow Art Theater had visited Yalta on tour. Andreeva was from a family with a strong interest in the arts (her father was director of the leading Petersburg theater), and at the turn of the century she was one of the most prominent actresses in Stanislavsky's troupe. Her involvement with Gorky and with political activity caused her to leave the Moscow Art Theater in 1904, though she returned briefly in 1905 to appear in *Children of the Sun*.[31] Owing to the difficulties of obtaining a divorce in Russia, Gorky was still legally married to Ekaterina Pavlovna. The two had parted on good terms, however: they continued to correspond regularly and Gorky supported both her and their two children.

His marital situation devastated his 1906 trip to the United States, where the Bolsheviks sent Gorky to gather money and support for the revolutionary cause. Public opinion in America was cool toward the tsarist government and sympathy for the 1905 insurgency was widespread: Gorky's arrest had aroused vigorous protests in the American press.[32] Prospects were bright for a successful visit. The committee in charge of the arrangements was chaired by Mark Twain and included Jane Addams, S. S. McClure, and William Dean Howells. A crowd of thousands met Gorky upon his arrival on 10 April, and for the first few days all went well. But then one of the New York newspapers, acting on a tip from the Russian embassy, broke the story that the woman with whom Gorky was traveling was not his legal wife. Even though Andreeva by then had been his common-law wife for over two years and their relationship was no secret, virtually no one in the United States had been aware of Gorky's marital situation. The revelation caused an uproar. Many of his public appearances had to be canceled, and the couple was evicted from several hotels. Gorky and Andreeva were then invited to the home of a well-to-do socialist who lived on Staten Island. There, and at that same family's vacation home in the Adirondacks, Gorky worked on his revolutionary novel *Mother* and wrote the play *Enemies,* as well as several pieces highly critical of the United States. Despite its scandalous beginning, the remainder of his stay in the United States gave him opportunity to write in relative peace, and he eventually had several meetings with prominent Americans. The idyllic summer, though, was saddened by the news of the death of Gorky's daughter, who had been living with her mother in Russia.

Early that fall Gorky and Andreeva left New York for Capri, where Gorky lived through 1913, one of the most productive periods of his career. In addition to several novels and some fine plays, he wrote *Childhood,* the first part of his autobiographical trilogy, which many consider his masterpiece. Gorky's literary talents fully matured during these years, when he was partly cut off from the political and literary life of Russia.

Gorky, however, maintained many connections with Russian lit-erary figures. Andreev, Bunin, and others visited him.[33] A steady stream of letters passed between him and his colleagues. He at-tempted to guide the fortunes of *Znanie* through Pyatnitsky, but growing political differences among the old *Sreda* members as well as Gorky's absence from Russia (which left the alliance without a strong leader) caused the publication's fortunes to wane. Many of the original contributors stopped writing for *Znanie* around 1909, and in 1911 Pyatnitsky assumed full legal control of what was already a failing operation, leaving Gorky no authority.[34]

Gorky's political involvement also remained strong, though his relationship with Lenin passed through a particularly difficult period. Much of the problem stemmed from Gorky's interest in "God-building," a movement combining religion and socialism. Several leading Marxists were behind it: Alexander Bogdanov, a leading Marxist philosopher, whose concern with the relationship between existence and consciousness gave rise to the trend of thought that culminated in God-building; Anatoly Lunacharsky, whose two-volume *Religion and Socialism* detected a strong socialist element in Christianity and described a religion of labor; and Gorky himself.[35] At about this time Gorky wrote the novel *A Confession*, which contains his most explicit presentation of socialism as a kind of religion, indeed a truer religion than that practiced by the Orthodox church. Some have viewed Gorky as heading in this direction even earlier, for instance in *The Lower Depths*, where in 1902, he expressed his faith in humanity in a way that foreshadows God-building.[36] Lenin had absolutely no patience with anything that smacked of religion, and on several occasions sharply criticized Gorky and the other God-builders. Another source of difficulties with Lenin was Gorky's effort to establish a school for Russian workers of revolutionary leanings. A group was recruited in Russia by an activist who returned there for the purpose, with the workers arriving on Capri in the summer of 1909. Bogdanov, Lunacharsky, Gorky, and others lectured the workers in their areas of expertise, but Lenin resolutely refused to participate since he regarded the school as a factionalist deviation. Eventually Lenin lured some of the workers to Paris, where he was living, for a series of corrective lectures, and Gorky's school soon closed.[37]

Although his writing ability was at a peak during these years, Gorky's literary reputation fluctuated. His political works composed in the United States (*Mother* and *Enemies*) received positive reviews from radical critics but were otherwise coolly received. His subsequent plays did not encounter an enthusiastic reception either, and the attitudes toward his novels depended at least in part on the critic's ideological position. But with what became known as his "Okurov Cycle" (*The Town of Okurov* and *The Life of Matvei Kozhemiakin*), which appeared serially from 1909 into 1911, his reputation slowly revived.[38] And *Childhood* restored Gorky's reputation as a, if not the, leading Russian prose writer of his day.

During 1913, as *Childhood* was still being written, word arrived of an amnesty granted in connection with the three hundredth anniversary of the Romanov dynasty. All those whose crimes consisted solely of writings judged seditious were pardoned. Though his crimes in fact extended beyond his writings, Gorky nonetheless took advantage of the amnesty to return to Russia at the very end of 1913 and among other things founded a journal called *Letopis'* [The Chronicle], which came out in Petrograd from late 1915 until the end of 1917. Its literature section offered prose by Gorky and Bunin, as well as works translated from foreign authors, while its commentaries went against the government's position by emphasizing the negative aspects of Russia's involvement in the First World War. Although the journal roughly followed the Bolshevik line (indeed Bolsheviks used it as a means for publishing their views legally), Lenin was dissatisfied with at least some of the stands it took. But Gorky's greatest conflicts with the Bolsheviks occurred through his editorship at the newspaper *Novaya zhizn'* [New Life], where he began writing a column "Untimely Thoughts" in the second issue of the paper, which was founded in April 1917, just two months after the tsar's abdication. At first Gorky concentrated on anti-war topics, with only occasional jabs at the Bolsheviks, but when Lenin's group seized power he began to express harsher attitudes. Despite his longtime association with the Bolshevik cause, he found the new regime too extreme and insufficiently respectful of the Russian culture it had inherited. His outspoken attacks continued until the paper was suppressed in the summer of 1918.[39]

Although Gorky remained suspicious of Bolshevik intentions, he soon began organizing efforts to help his fellow writers. Along with *Novaya zhizn'*, all other opposition newspapers and magazines were closed during mid-1918, so that writers found their opportunities for publishing quite limited. Subsequent months brought further hardships: a paper shortage almost stopped book publication for a while, and shortages of food and firewood plagued everyone in the cities.[40] Gorky's great achievements during the period 1918–1921 were, first of all, to arrange publishing ventures for both established and new writers; second, to help writers obtain food and shelter; and third, to intercede on behalf of writers who found themselves in trouble with the authorities.

Before the revolution Gorky, along with A. N. Tikhonov and I. P. Ladyzhnikov, had formed the *Parus* [The Sail] publishing house, which flourished from 1915 until early 1918. In the summer of 1918 these three men, along with Z. I. Grzhebin, who had joined *Parus* in 1916, signed an agreement among themselves to organize *Vsemirnaya literatura* [World Literature]. The goal of the new venture was to publish classics of foreign literature written since the second half of the eighteenth century. Talent was available: the editors for the volumes on Western literatures included Gorky, the poets Alexander Blok and Nikolai Gumilev, and the critic Kornei Chukovsky. Gorky's plans were ambitious: he intended to create a "Basic Library" of fifteen hundred books and a "Popular Library" with between three and five thousand titles. But the paper shortages of the civil war period, disputes with the State Publishing House, and Gorky's own departure from the Soviet Union in 1921 made these goals unattainable. At the time he left only fifty-nine volumes had appeared, and when *Vsemirnaya literatura* went out of business in 1924 its catalogue contained just over two hundred titles.[41]

The very existence of *Vsemirnaya literatura* was nonetheless instrumental in bringing writers together and in maintaining the cultural life of Petrograd during the years immediately following the revolution. The editors decided that if the publishing house were to translate or retranslate most of the world's classics from the past century and a half, it would be desirable to organize a literary studio where theories of translation could be tested and if necessary reformulated in the course of actual work. Chukovsky and Gumilev published a pamphlet on literary translation, and in February 1919 a workshop was opened.[42] Among the students were half a dozen young writers who eventually helped form the group known as the Serapion Brothers: Mikhail Zoshchenko, Mikhail Slonimsky, Lev Lunts, Elizaveta Polonskaya, Vladimir Pozner, and Ilya Gruzdev (who became Gorky's biographer).[43]

While translation projects created immediate work for writers, Gorky was interested in publishing Russian literature as well. He was part of a loosely organized (and soon disbanded) group called the Union of Belletrists, which in early 1919 nominally included most of Petrograd's best writers—Gorky, Blok, Gumilev, Zamyatin, and Kuprin were all members. All were part of his *Vsemirnaya literatura* venture, and all were on the proposed editorial staff for a new publishing venture that was to issue works by contemporary writers.[44] Clearly the one was to be adjunct to the other. But conflicts between the editorial staff and the governing board of the Union of Belletrists soon proved irresolvable, and the project collapsed.

At the same time it was necessary to provide for writers materially and also locate more or less permanent quarters where they could meet and carry on their work. At the end of 1919 the House of the Arts *(Dom iskusstv,* known to its inhabitants by the acronym *Disk)* was set up in a huge building near the center of Petrograd.[45] The center established there attracted most of the students and teachers from the *Vsemirnaya literatura* studio, for *Disk,* besides offering shelter and access to rations, permitted writers to concentrate on Russian literature and avoid the orientation toward foreign literatures at *Vsemirnaya literatura. Disk* served as the home for the emerging group of Serapion Brothers, and also provided a full schedule of special lectures as well as courses on various aspects of literature and the arts.[46]

At about that time Gorky was instrumental in creating the Scholars' House *(Dom uchenykh).* The Commission to Improve Scholars' Living Conditions, headed in Petrograd by Gorky, established an "academic ration," which was distributed to scholars in all fields through the *Dom uchenykh.*[47] Thanks again to Gorky's efforts, writers and artists were included with scholars on the list of those eligible for the ration. Not long after Gorky left Russia *Disk* was closed down, but the Scholars' House continues to function in its original location to this day, and it spawned other Scholars' Houses in various places throughout the Soviet Union.

In addition to his tireless organizational efforts, Gorky also took a close personal interest in the lives and works of writers. Konstantin Fedin, a Serapion, has detailed Gorky's attentiveness throughout his memoir, appropriately titled *Gorky among Us,* recalling at one point Gorky's insistence on learning the precise details of how Fedin went about his writing.[48] Gorky's willingness, even need, to give advice appears in his early correspondence with another Serapion, Venyamin Kaverin. While still in Petrograd he carefully measured his praise and criticism for Kaverin's first stories, finding them unclear, too "literary," but "almost" talented; he urged the young writer to learn from experience.[49] A bit later, writing Kaverin from abroad, Gorky advised him to maintain close ties with his fellow Serapions but to ignore what he called "speculators in the beautiful but empty word"—

that is, those who pay too much attention to style for its own sake.[50]
For the most part writers appear to have appreciated Gorky's attention, but some were suspicious. In his memoir *A Sentimental Journey,* Viktor Shklovsky, himself a kind of godfather to the Serapions and a prominent formalist critic, acknowledged Gorky's great service as the "Noah" of the Russian intelligentsia, whose "ark" saved Shklovsky himself and the Serapions generally from the ravages of the civil war years. At the same time Shklovsky was bothered by Gorky's insistence on forcing all of world literature into a schema; he found in this methodological approach something reminiscent of Lenin.[51]

At least in those days Gorky himself still had some doubts about the revolution. His *Novaya zhizn'* articles were still fresh in his memory, and his efforts to help writers brought him into frequent conflict with the authorities. In 1921 he failed to save Gumilev from execution for participation in what appears to have been a counterrevolutionary plot. He often clashed with Grigory Zinovev, the head of the Petrograd Communist Party committee and a longtime associate of Lenin's. In 1921 Lenin advised Gorky to go abroad for his health. While Gorky was certainly not robust, the reasons for his departure may well have been more complex. Possibly Lenin was unhappy with Gorky's constant petitions on behalf of writers, possibly the conflict with Zinovev had taken a more serious turn.[52] In any case, that October Gorky left for Germany via Finland and did not set foot on Russian soil for nearly seven years.

European Interlude and Return

By then another change had occurred in Gorky's personal life. Upon her return to Russia from Capri ahead of Gorky, Maria Andreeva had resumed her acting career. While the two remained close, their paths began to diverge over the next several years. After the revolution Gorky met Moura Budberg, then about twenty-seven, who had already led an adventurous life including involvement with the acting British ambassador to Russia, Robert Bruce Lockhart. Later she was close to H. G. Wells. Although she spoke several languages fluently and worked as a Russian-English translator, her Russian sounded strangely foreign. Her unusual qualities—from her poor Russian to her fearless behavior to her readiness to discuss any topic—attracted many, including Gorky. With some difficulty

Gorky managed to get her out of Russia; once abroad she was with him throughout his stay in Germany, and later accompanied him to Italy. Although she declined to return to Russia when he did, she continued to translate his works and maintained contact with him even after he had settled in the Soviet Union.[53]

Whatever the state of Gorky's health, he quickly resumed his publishing activities once in Germany. He worked on both a journal and series called *Chronicle of the Revolution* [*Letopis' Revoliutsii*], which published various materials connected with the history of the Russian revolutionary movement. The others most active in the endeavor were largely Mensheviks—i.e., from the wing of the Social Democrats opposed to Lenin's Bolshevik group.[54] Gorky's participation in the *Chronicle*, although brief, nonetheless may indicate something about his feelings toward the Bolsheviks at the time. Gorky's chief efforts, though, were devoted to the journal *Beseda (Dialogue)*, which he founded along with the poet Vladislav Khodasevich. In the early 1920s it still seemed possible—even likely—that journals published abroad would be allowed into Russia and Gorky was reasonably sure that a journal of his would be sold within the Soviet Union. But his hopes proved vain, and the effort soon floundered.[55]

After a short interval in Czechoslovakia Gorky returned to Italy, living in Sorrento. He remained there until his 1928 trip to Russia and thereafter visited the Soviet Union regularly until he moved back permanently in 1933.[56] In all Gorky spent at least parts of eighteen years in Italy; over half his literary work was done on Capri or in Sorrento. His second stay, though, occurred under more complex personal and political conditions than his first. Italy was no longer a very hospitable place for a writer (no matter how famous) with left-wing leanings. Mussolini's fascist government was already in power; Gorky himself was not seriously bothered by officials, but foreigners who came to see him sometimes were.[57] In addition, Gorky was under great pressure from various sides. Many émigrés wanted him to come out more strongly against the Bolshevik government, while others simply mistrusted his motives altogether. The Soviet government made constant efforts to secure his return. Khodasevich notes that when Gorky's first wife, Ekaterina Pavlovna, visited him in 1925, she seemed to have contacts high in the Kremlin and constantly praised the accomplishments of the Soviets.[58] The American Slavist Alexander Kaun, visiting Gorky to gather material for a biography, noted a different kind of distraction. He compared the villa in Sorrento to Tolstoy's estate, Yasnaya Polyana, where the great writer had received a steady stream of guests.[59] Gorky was also the object of much attention, receiving frequent visits from major European writers as well as from those able to come from Russia—such as Olga Forsh, a historical novelist, and the young Leonid Leonov and Valentin Kataev.

Despite these frequent interruptions, Gorky's years abroad were quite productive. From 1917 through 1921, while still in Russia, he had completed a few works, including some of his excellent literary memoirs. On the whole, though, he wrote relatively little during the immediate postrevolutionary era, when he was totally absorbed in assisting his fellow writers. Soon after arriving in Germany he resumed work on his autobiographical writings, completing the third part of his trilogy, *My Universities (Moi universitety)*, as well as a series of memoirs. During the same period he also worked on the items that later constituted *Fragments from a Diary (Zametki iz dnevnika)* and on the tales collected under the title *Stories of 1922–1924 (Rasskazy 1922–1924 godov)*. During the mid-1920s he completed *The Artamonov Business (Delo Artamonovykh)*, a novel he had begun before the revolution, and he started working on what was to be the longest work of his career, *The Life of Klim Samgin*, the fourth and final volume of which remained uncomplete at the time of Gorky's death. The early work on the novel, done while Gorky was still living abroad, went rapidly; his progress slowed only after he began to visit the Soviet Union again.

Gorky found it difficult to write about the revolution or its aftermath; his final novels end with 1917, after extensive treatments of the entire prerevolutionary era. The historical character of his work led to comments that the younger generation would not understand Gorky, a critique he accepted, adding that the older generation no doubt simply would not like him.[60] In October of 1927, on the thirty-fifth anniversary of Gorky's literary debut, a serious discussion took place in the Soviet Union as to whether Gorky could be considered a true proletarian writer: his concentration on prerevolutionary themes and his tendency toward romanticism brought his standing into question. This debate, which occurred only a few months before Gorky's celebrated return to the Soviet Union, was resolved in his favor.[61]

Gorky's decision to visit the Soviet Union in 1928 was a distinct departure from his outlook of the early 1920s. He had left his homeland at a time when travel abroad was not yet severely restricted. Many of those then living in western Europe were still debating whether to go back—and some did. Further, at least publicly, Gorky left at Lenin's behest for reasons of health; thus the doors were no doubt always open to his return. But the attitudes expressed in his letters were often as hostile as anything he had written in his "Untimely Thoughts" of 1917 and 1918. He protested vigorously against a trial of Socialist Revolutionaries, saying that their execution would amount to premeditated murder.[62] He wrote Khodasevich that if a rumored "guide for removing counter-revolutionary literature" should indeed exist in the Soviet Union, he would have to renounce his citizenship.[63] As time elapsed, though, his feelings toward the Soviet Union softened. He was deeply moved by Lenin's death and afterward recalled their relations nostalgically, and stressed the better sides of the Bolsheviks.[64] Then too family concerns mounted. Ekaterina Pavlovna may have failed to persuade him to return, but there was their son Maxim, who lived with his family with Gorky in Italy. All agree that Maxim was intelligent and good-natured but also immature and condemned to live in his father's shadow. Gorky's worries about his son's behavior were a frequent topic of his letters.[65] Khodasevich reports a conversation from which it appears that Maxim had earlier worked for the secret police, the Cheka; there are other indications he did so again when he was back in Russia.[66] In any case Gorky may well have felt a need to help his son, who, as it turned out, was to die in 1934—apparently, though not certainly, of natural causes. The chief reason for Gorky's return, though, may well be the one Khodasevich cites: the poet stresses the importance to Gorky of everything he had struggled for and of the role he had created for himself as bard of the revolution and of the proletariat. Giving up that ideal, and consequently calling into question the significance of his entire life, would have been more than he could bear.[67]

Gorky's sixtieth birthday, in March 1928, was celebrated throughout the Soviet Union, as the way was prepared for his return two months later. Gorky stayed in the Soviet Union until October of that year, receiving honors and congratulations at every turn. Over the next several years he divided his time between his own country and Italy. Some Soviet sources say that he actually settled in Moscow in 1931, and that his next two trips to Sorrento were taken solely for reasons of health.[68] In any case, during 1931 and

1932 he was abroad about as much as he was in the Soviet Union. He returned permanently only from May 1933 on. During his last years Gorky scarcely slowed down. His literary output suffered from his frequent trips to Italy, as well as from the official duties he assumed in the Soviet Union. Gorky made countless speeches and appearances, and he wrote numerous articles in support of the regime: for example, he coedited a volume of articles praising the White Sea Canal project and extolling the use of imprisoned laborers as a successful attempt at "rehabilitation."[69] He also maintained an active interest in various publishing houses, corresponding regularly with the chief editors and pressing for the publication of works he considered important.[70] His skill at literary politics made him instrumental in the establishment of the Writers' Union, which, whatever its failings, started as an effort to improve the situation of writers: certainly for most the union was an improvement over its predecessor organizations. In 1934 he gave the opening address at the first congress of the union and was elected chairman of the congress. By then he was the acknowledged "father" of Soviet literature and the writer whose works provided some of the chief models for socialist realism, the method then officially proclaimed as obligatory for Soviet writers.

The extent to which Gorky's ongoing concern for his fellow writers might have brought him into conflict with powerful political figures of the day is not clear. On the surface all went well, and he gathered honors and awards. In 1932 his hometown of Nizhny Novgorod was renamed Gorky. The chief literary institute in Moscow was named in his honor, as was one of the city's main streets. Libraries, schools, and theaters all over the country came to bear his name. But then the assassination of the Leningrad party leader Sergei Kirov at the end of 1934 marked the beginning of tensions that culminated in the purges of the late 1930s. Gorky's health had long been poor, so that his serious illness in the spring of 1936 was hardly a surprise, nor was his death on 18 June. He received full state honors and his ashes were buried in the Kremlin wall. Nearly two years later, though, at one of the purge trials it was claimed that Gorky had been murdered by Genrikh Yagoda (in 1936 still head of the secret police) and several accomplices, including Gorky's doctors.

After Stalin's death Soviet publications again began to say that Gorky had died of natural causes, but the questions raised by the initial charge have not subsided. As with Kirov, now widely considered to have been murdered on Stalin's orders, many wonder whether in fact Gorky was killed. Khodasevich, writing during the trial of the supposed assassins, still felt that Gorky's poor health made the original story of a natural death more likely.[71] A defector and former official in the Soviet secret police has likewise concluded that the alleged "plot" was a fabrication.[72] In a recent book Nina Berberova, the widow of Khodasevich, examines much of the evidence that has come out in recent years but finds no convincing proof that Gorky was murdered.[73] And yet enough questions remain to prevent our reaching a definite conclusion. Thus Gorky in death as in life remains an enigma.

Chapter Two
Literary Beginnings: The Short Story

Romantic Tales

Gorky's stories have been partially eclipsed in the popular imagination by his novels, plays, and autobiographical writings; and yet include some of his finest achievements. Of particular importance for an understanding of his literary career are his stories of the 1890s. These, his first published works, introduced new themes, new heroes, and new attitudes to Russian literature. What is more, Gorky developed his literary techniques within the genre of the short story and then applied them in his other fictional (and even some nonfictional) writings.

No less important than their subject matter and form is the role that Gorky's stories played in establishing his literary reputation. During the 1880s and 1890s the short story became a major genre for a number of writers—beginning with Vsevelod Garshin, continuing with Chekhov, and going on to writers of what might, roughly speaking, be called Gorky's generation: Ivan Bunin, Alexander Kuprin, Leonid Andreev, and many others. But none of them had such an overwhelming early success as Gorky. A two-volume collection, *Sketches and Stories,* was published in 1898, just six years after his first story had appeared. A third volume came out in 1899, followed that year by a second edition of the complete set. The *Znanie* publishing house issued a new four-volume collection in 1900, and for some time thereafter new and ever larger editions appeared at an average rate of more than one per year.[1] Total sales of Gorky's books soon reached the unprecedented figure of one hundred thousand.[2] Thus even before he became known for his novels and plays, Gorky had achieved a literary fame that enabled him also to emerge at the beginning of the century as an influential social activist.

Gorky's first published story, "Makar Chudra" (1892), may initially seem quite different from his subsequent writings. The tale describes the Gypsy Loiko Zobar, a fearless young man and talented musician, and Radda, the fiercely independent young woman with whom he falls in love. After a great deal of difficulty, Loiko succeeds in getting Radda to declare her love for him, but she insists he submit to her before she will become his wife. Torn between his love and his equally strong desire for freedom, Loiko kills her and is killed in turn by Radda's father. The story contains many romantic elements: exotic descriptions of the Gypsies, highly idealized central figures, and a love intrigue with an almost predictably tragic outcome. All this seems very far from the Gorky who describes the homeless wanderers of Russia's lower depths or the corrupt members of middle-class society.

Yet upon closer examination the romantic elements turn out to owe much to Gorky's interest in folk legends, which went back to the tales he heard from his grandmother. Loiko and Radda were, according to Gorky's own testimony, based on folk legends he had heard. "Makar Chudra" also borrows from folklore many of the metaphors and turns of phrase that distinguish its characters' speech.[3] Indeed, virtually the whole tale is written in highly stylized language—either that of the lovers or of Makar Chudra, who relates their story to the narrator.

The narration is quite typical for Gorky's stories of the 1890s. The first-person narrator says virtually nothing about himself; after offering a brief description of the setting and of the old Gypsy Makar Chudra, he largely disappears, except for one or two subsequent comments about Makar and a short return at the end of the story. For the most part, then, the words are those of Makar Chudra, who praises the narrator for wandering about and seeing what he can of life. Others are not concerned with you, feels Makar, and you cannot teach others. The only thing to do is wander and be free. With that as a preface, the story he tells about the Gypsy lovers becomes a cautionary tale, an illustration of his own philosophy. The narrator simply listens; it is not clear what he, or Gorky, believes.

A story similar in form to "Makar Chudra" is "Old Izergil" ("Starukha Izergil'," 1894). Both take place by the sea and consist of tales told the narrator by an older person, whose name is also that of the story. The non-Russian characters, the exotic settings, and the influence of folk legends contribute to these works' predominantly romantic aura. "Old Izergil," however, is by far the more complex of the two and gives evidence of Gorky's increasing maturity. Generally a harsh critic of his own writing, Gorky was always to feel that "Old Izergil" was among his very best creations.[4] Old Izergil relates not one tale but three. The first describes Larra, the humanlike offspring of an eagle and a woman, who kills a maiden after she refuses to marry him. Larra is then cut off from human contact and forced to live forever with his guilt. In the third, equally fantastic, tale, a tribe has hidden from its enemies by migrating to the depths of a swampy forest. A young member of the tribe, Danko, tries to lead his people out. The journey is difficult, and when the others rebel against his leadership, he tears his burning heart from his breast and by its light leads them to freedom before he dies. Sandwiched between the two legends is the earthy story of Izergil's own life, with its succession of loves and adventures.

The structure of "Old Izergil" seems awkward at first. The first and third tales appear to have little to do with the second, while the account of Izergil's romantic escapades contrasts with the fourth portion of the story, scenes in which the narrator and Izergil, by now an old crone, talk directly. But this lack of any obvious cohesiveness turns out to be a strength. The work's theme emerges less from direct statement, as in Makar Chudra's monologue, than through the juxtaposition of quite different plots. The resultant "disunity" is a favorite device of the mature Gorky; in somewhat less blatant form this approach is responsible for the relatively unimportant role that single, unifying plot lines play in his longer stories. The significance of the entire work must be constructed out of its disparate parts. Even "Makar Chudra," where the one-sided dialogue of the opening pages seems at first only loosely related to what follows, utilizes this technique in embryonic form. Only in "Old Izergil," however, is it first employed to full effect.

The two legendary episodes in "Old Izergil" modify the emphasis on freedom seen in "Makar Chudra." To be sure, both Larra and Danko are strong individuals who stand above those around them, but here Gorky stresses their ties to others. Larra cannot kill another with impunity, and his very punishment consists of exile from human contact. Danko tears out his heart not to assert his independence, but as a way of helping his community, at the cost of his life.

How do the tales relate to Izergil herself? As if following Makar Chudra's advice, Izergil had wandered about, but her life ultimately lacks the romantic qualities of the legends she relates. She was proud and valued freedom, yet she lacked constancy or any goal beyond her own pleasure.[5] As she grew older her conquests faded: in her last affair she was the one abandoned. She has spent the last thirty years of her life in Moldavia, where she did once have a husband, but that entire period means little to her. Her willfulness and the punishment that life has dealt her recall Larra's fate, while Danko is the model she should have followed. Izergil has failed to give meaning to her life.

Allegorical Tales

Throughout the 1890s and later Gorkʸ wrote many works that may be described as "programmatic"—that is, they state his views on life and literature more directly than his ordinary fiction. Not surprisingly, these works tend to be allegorical, and several of them, like "Makar Chudra" and "Old Izergil," employ folk motifs. The earliest is called "About the Siskin Who Lied and the Woodpecker Who Loved the Truth" ("O chizhe, kotoryi lgal, i o diatle—liubitele istiny," 1892). It describes a grove where all the birds, oppressed by the gloomy weather, sing only songs of despair until a single bird turns to "bold songs of freedom." Their spirits lifted, the other birds fly toward the singer, who, it develops, is but a lowly siskin. Though taken aback, they still want to fly off to what the siskin's song promises is a land of happiness until a woodpecker interrupts to claim he possesses the truth while the siskin's songs are nothing but a lie (1:51). The woodpecker's speech, full of solemn formality and bureaucratic jargon, contrasts both with the siskin's songs, presented in rhymed iambic tetrameter verse, and with the siskin's impassioned plea to his fellow birds. The woodpecker maintains that the siskin's songs have no basis in reality, and the other birds return to their places, leaving the siskin alone.

The most important theme of the story—and an important concern for Gorky throughout his career—is the nature of truth.[6] For Gorky, the truth is not necessarily good, and lies are not always bad. Anything that reconciles people to a life that is unjust or less rich than it could be is bad; anything, whether truth or falsehood, that causes them to seek a change for the better is good. The siskin is a romantic, perhaps even a revolutionary. He wants the birds to seek happiness in another land. The woodpecker, who feeds on worms and finds his inspiration in dry facts, is a forerunner of the merchants and other middle-class figures in Gorky's stories who fight for the status quo. A similar message is conveyed by the "Song of the Falcon" ("Pesnia o Sokole," 1894), sung to the narrator by a Crimean shepherd named Rahim. He tells of a grass snake that is crawling in a high gorge above the sea when a mortally wounded falcon falls nearby. The falcon tells the snake of the wonderful life he has lived and in a last effort to fly falls to his death in the sea. The snake, curious, tries to fly as well. He crashes harmlessly on some rocks beneath a cliff and concludes that his earthbound existence is superior to flight.[7] The falcon and the snake are analogous to the siskin and the woodpecker from Gorky's earlier tale; the difference is that the falcon tells not an inspirational lie but the truth.

The animals in the "Song of the Falcon," as Betty Forman has demonstrated, also resemble the eagle and the serpent in a parable from Nietzsche's "Thus Spake Zarathustra."[8] The general question of Nietzsche's influence on Gorky is complex and has been the subject of much discussion. Not long after the turn of the century Gorky rejected most of Nietzsche's teaching (though even after the revolution he borrowed the title *Untimely Thoughts* for his own essays), and by the time he wrote *The Life of Klim Samgin* he referred to him only disparagingly.[9] Yet it is equally true that critics of Gorky's own time saw much in Gorky that struck them as Nietzschean, even in some of his positive characters. His emphasis on daring and inner strength, the extent to which his heroes are individualists opposed to the rest of society, and his harsh condemnation of bourgeois society—all parallel Nietzsche's views. Certainly Gorky's falcon, who dies in an effort to regain his freedom, could be seen as a Nietzschean protagonist.

In 1901 Gorky published another allegory employing folk motifs, his "Song of the Stormy Petrel" ("Pesnia o Burevestnike"). The stormy petrel as a metaphor of social unrest and a possible harbinger of revolution has literary antecedents in nineteenty-century Russia as well.[10] But, after the publication of this work in the Marxist journal *Zhizn'*, subsequently shut down by the authorities, that association became even stronger. On occasion the phrase was attached to Gorky himself.[11] If the siskin told courageous lies and was ultimately defeated, if the falcon died even as he proclaimed the truth, then the stormy petrel says nothing but soars boldly and triumphantly over the other creatures. The "program" behind this and Gorky's other allegories is the need to envision a better, loftier existence in the inevitable future.

Not all Gorky's allegorical tales contain folk motifs. Several—including "The Reader" ("Chitatel'," 1895–98), "About the Devil" ("O cherte," 1898), and "More about the Devil" ("Eshche o cherte," 1899)—employ fantasy, along with a degree of whimsy, to make a statement about the writer's role in society. In "The Reader" an author is accosted one night by a mysterious reader, who asks whether his interlocutor has fulfilled the duties of a writer. According to the reader, the "goal of literature is to help man understand himself, to strengthen his belief in himself, and to develop in him a striving for the truth" (4:115–16).

The Vagabonds

The narrator in "Makar Chudra," "Old Izergil," and "Song of the Falcon" may tentatively be identified with Gorky himself, whose journeys throughout Russia in the years before he began publishing had taken him to the Ukraine, the Crimea, the Caucasus, and other regions depicted in his stories. This traveler does not focus attention upon himself: after describing the setting he allows someone else to relate a tale. In other works, though, the focus is precisely on the wanderer, a person outside society, who comes sometimes from the lower classes, sometimes from the better-educated strata of Russian society. This hero—the *bosiak* or vagabond—no longer feels beholden to others. He seeks to live on his own, by his own rules. Gorky felt that neither the urban intelligentsia nor the peasantry could provide guidance in the search for a better society: individuals must begin anew, breaking with old customs and rules. The *bosiak* rejects the indecisiveness of the educated classes as well as the submissiveness of the peasantry. He is not troubled by guilt and is willing to take what he feels is rightfully his. More than any other single element, the somewhat romanticized image of the vagabond was responsible for the immense popularity that Gorky's stories achieved after the first two volumes of his *Sketches and Stories* were published. The *bosiak* struck Gorky's contemporaries as a radically new type of literary hero, one with whom a large portion of the reading public could sympathize.[12]

Upon examination Gorky's vagabond turns out to be a complex

and often ambiguous figure. This is true even of "Chelkash" (1894), Gorky's first extensive treatment of the type. Grishka Chelkash is a well-known thief in a large port city, evidently Odessa. His usual accomplice has a broken leg, and so he takes on Gavrila, a young peasant, newly arrived from the country. The robbery that Chelkash has planned goes off smoothly, but at the end of the story a confrontation takes place between Chelkash and Gavrila over the loot. At the story's conclusion each goes his own way.

The critical moment occurs during the final scene. On several earlier occasions violence almost erupts, but each time the situation eases. Just when all danger seems past Gavrila and Chelkash have their altercation. Gavrila has mentioned earlier how much the money would mean to him, and Chelkash gives Gavrila 40 rubles out of the 540 he has been paid for the loot. When Gavrila literally begs for the rest of it, Chelkash contemptuously hands it over, but forcibly takes it back when Gavrila admits that he had thought of killing his partner to obtain all the money. As Chelkash walks away, Gavrila hits him on the head with a rock and then runs off without taking anything back. A short while later he returns, asks Chelkash's forgiveness, and is given most of the money. Gavrila then departs for the country while Chelkash returns to the city.

Without a doubt the peasant comes off worse in the exchange. Each of his actions—begging for the money, hurling the rock, even returning to seek forgiveness—is motivated by a combination of greed and cowardice. Gavrila's ties to his land and his family, traits that have traditionally been powerful in the Russian peasant, only cause an able young man to commit unworthy acts. No wonder that the Populist critics, who saw the future of Russia embodied in the peasantry, disliked the story.

"Chelkash" contains more than a conflict between peasant and vagabond. As is typical for the early Gorky, the story is introduced by a lengthy description of the bustle, cacophony, and oppressiveness of the daily routine in a busy port. The massive ships and machinery dwarf the individual. Chelkash's thievery could be justified as a kind of protest against the reigning order, though Chelkash himself would hardly analyze his actions in such lofty terms. No less important is the depiction of Chelkash. In the opening description he is, suitably for a *bosiak,* barefoot *(bos),* but the adjective applied to him most frequently is *khishchnyi* (rapacious or grasping). The word is most often applied to a bird of prey, which Chelkash is said to resemble, though here it is also used to describe his face, his nose, and even his leanness (2:9). Within the same passage he is said to be like a hawk (as in Gorky's allegorical stories, birds are associated with freedom), while the other animals mentioned—wolf, cat—are also significant.

The great care Gorky gave to this and other descriptions is evident from the extensive revisions he made even after the story's original publication. "Chelkash" is not unique in this regard; throughout his life Gorky constantly revised his published works. In the case of his earlier writings he was very likely responding at least in part to what he himself came to view as stylistic excesses, a fault criticized by Chekhov, among others. In a letter to Gorky of 3 December 1898, Chekhov commented on Gorky's collected stories published that year. He praised Gorky's natural talents, but also noted some deficiencies in his writing: "I'll begin with the fact that in my opinion you lack restraint. You are like a spectator in a theater who expresses his ecstasy so unrestrainedly that he keeps himself and others from hearing. This lack of restraint is especially evident in your descriptions of nature, with which you interrupt dialogues. When you read these descriptions you wish that they were more compact, some two or three lines shorter."[13] Chekhov also notes Gorky's overuse of such words as languor, whispering, velvetiness; his lack of restraint in depicting women; and the absence of naturalness in his more sophisticated characters. Thus, in reworking "Chelkash" Gorky attempted to correct his tendency to overwrite. For example, while Chelkash is committing the robbery, Gavrila sits surrounded by silence. Originally Gorky elaborated in some detail on the terrible nature of that silence, but later he greatly shortened the passage.[14] Throughout the story Gorky abbreviated descriptions, most often by removing unnecessary adjectives and adverbs.[15] In all, the final version, while lacking the conciseness of a Chekhov story, is clearly a better written and more effective tale than it was originally.

Gorky's works depicting vagabonds often contain a marked autobiographical element. In a letter to his Russian biographer, Ilya Gruzdev, he remarked that the name Chelkash came from a fowler, while the plot of the story was based on a tale he had heard from a *bosiak*.[16] Gorky's experiences are reflected in other works written during the 1890s, where the focus is on the interaction between a *bosiak* and the narrator: examples include "A Rolling Stone" ("Prokhodimets," 1898) and "Konovalov" (1896). But if earlier the narrator was largely a passive listener, in these he appears as an active participant.

The narrator of "A Rolling Stone" meets Promtov on a wretched night when both have failed to find shelter in a village. An aggressive beggar, Promtov lies, steals, and frightens people to get his way. After they have spent several days together, he tells the narrator his life story. He came from a good family but was a misfit from the start. Although he had no difficulty in attracting women and acquiring money, he more or less by chance fell into the life of a vagabond when he was exiled from Saint Petersburg after a misadventure. He discovers that he likes being a *bosiak:* "It's pleasant to feel yourself free from obligations, from the various little bonds that tie you down when you are among people"(4:52). Promtov rejoices not only in his freedom to wander about, but also in his ability to fool people; he has turned all of life into a game.

While Chelkash, a former peasant and a thief, nonetheless displays the romantic aura of the underdog who flouts authority, Promtov is calculating and cynical in his view of the world. Gorky, writing much later when his anti-Nietzschean opinions had been clearly formed, claimed that in Promtov and similar characters he had purposely embodied what he regarded as Nietzschean qualities.[17] In depicting such figures Gorky substantially modified the unquestioning admiration of strength evident in his portrayal of Loiko Zobar and Danko. Vigor, determination, and independence are still positive traits for Gorky, but his vagabonds can display negative characteristics as well. Their chief merit lies in their rejection of contemporary bourgeois society; they themselves are not necessarily ideal personalities.[18]

Nor is the vagabond always presented as a strong figure. Gorky's Kazan period of the 1880s, especially his bakery work, is recorded in the third part of his autobiographical trilogy, *My Universities;* those years also provide the background for his long autobiographical story "The Boss" ("Khoziain") and for two of his best fictional pieces from the 1890s: "Creatures That Once Were Men" ("Byvshie liudi") and "Twenty-Six Men and a Girl" ("Dvadtsat' shest' i odna"). Taken as a whole, his "Kazan cycle" represents some of his very best writing.

Plot is of secondary importance in "Konovalov," named for a Kazan baker with whom Gorky worked. If Gorky's recollections are accurate, the structure of the story mirrors the sequence of real-life events on which the story is based. At the outset the narrator (i.e., Gorky) reads about the suicide of Konovalov. He then attempts to explain what might have led to his sad end by first recalling the period when the two worked together and then describing a chance meeting with him sometime afterward in Feodosia.[19] Events are largely undramatic; description prevails over narration. Also, the transition between the two scenes is abrupt (as indeed are the transitions in many of Gorky's longer works, including "Chelkash" and "A Rolling Stone"), and at first the sections seem only loosely connected.

The Konovalov of the first, much longer section is a baker who clearly loves his work. The narrator admires Konovalov's ability to wield huge amounts of dough and to bake batch after batch of bread to perfection. Books fascinate Konovalov, who enjoys having the narrator read to him. A novella by Fedor Reshetnikov (1841–71), a chronicler of the rural and urban poor, produces a great effect on Konovalov, as does an historical account of the seventeenth-century uprising led by the cossack Stenka Razin. The baker is less taken by Dostoevsky's first work, Poor People—not surprisingly given Gorky's antipathy toward Dostoevsky. The narrator tells Konovalov about the hard life of writers, and Konovalov sees their sensitivity to life as resulting in a misery that they attempt to purge through drink (3:22). What he says about writers largely applies to himself as well. He has a reputation as a drunkard, and even though he works for a while, eventually he goes on another spree before disappearing from Kazan. Earlier he had spoken of himself as a person who is sometimes so overwhelmed by misery that he feels he cannot go on living. His relations with women are characteristic. He has been close to more than one, but each time he falls into a depression and leaves her. The arrival in Kazan of one young woman he had helped earlier leads directly to the drinking bout that causes him to quit work. He simply cannot shoulder the burden of another's attention. At the same time he blames only himself for his failings: his brother, who had the same upbringing, has made much more of his life. In a moment of despair he says that people like himself do not deserve to live.[20]

When the narrator comes across him in the second part of the story, Konovalov is working as a construction worker on a breakwater on the Crimean coast. At first Konovalov seems to be healthier and happier for having roamed about for the preceding few years, but the narrator realizes that he is still unhappy, still searching for something. Gorky ties together the story's two seemingly disparate sections with a series of parallels. Konovalov's interest in books has not faded, and he has continued to attract women and then abandon them. But the later meeting illuminates the earlier portion in another way as well. When Konovalov and the narrator converse, they are within sight of the calm sea. At the same time their conversation is hampered by the chattering teeth and convulsive movements of a sick vagabond who is staying with Konovalov. The two live in a cave on a hill, just beneath a large boulder that would crush them if it fell. The oppressive and immediate presence of illness and death contrasts with the beauty of the distant sea. The scene evokes the misery that has always dwelled within Konovalov as well as the peace he has sought but cannot attain.

Naturalistic Tales

In classifying Gorky's position among writers of the turn of the century, Russian critics have most often referred to him as a *critical realist,* a term used to describe authors who wrote realistic stories incorporating a critical attitude toward the society of their day.[21] In some of Gorky's works, though, any criticism of society is more implicit than explicit. Such stories portray, in a seemingly neutral manner, the harshness that often exists in human beings and in nature itself.

Two such works—"On a Raft" ("Na plotakh," 1898) and "In the Steppe" ("V stepi," 1897)—are among Gorky's darkest, and also among Chekhov's favorites.[22] In the first tale Silan Petrov has taken away his son's wife. While the son talks with another worker at the back of a raft, Silan and his daughter-in-law embrace at the front. "In the Steppe" is narrated by one of three hungry tramps who come across an ill man with food. They first ask for some of the food, then take the rest by force. In the middle of the night one of the three kills the sick traveler, robs him, and leaves. The other two wake up, discover what has happened, and hastily depart.

What attracted Chekhov to such works? In the first place, they are among Gorky's most concise, most harmoniously composed stories. The first-person narrator is absent, except at the very end of "In the Steppe," and perhaps for that reason there is less description, less effort to set a mood. The atmosphere is established by the events, which begin immediately, and by the dialogue. In addition, with the exception of the final lines of "In the Steppe," Gorky avoids the moralistic or philosophical passages that sometimes mar even his best works. Instead, the ideas emerge in the course of the action.

Much longer and more complex are "Cain and Artyom" ("Kain i Artem," 1898) and "Malva" (1897), two of a group of works from the late 1890s in which Gorky develops insoluble conflicts between characters whose makeup is too different to allow them to understand one another. The dilemmas are reminiscent of those often experienced by better-educated or at least better-bred people in the works of other Russian writers. Part of Gorky's originality is to transpose such psychological dramas to situations involving people who are less knowledgeable and relatively incapable of self-analysis.[23]

Artyom is a handsome, powerful, but lazy bully of twenty-five who lives on handouts he receives from his many female admirers. One night several of Artyom's enemies set upon him when he is drunk, beat him, and leave him for dead. After being nursed back to health by Cain, a Jewish ragman who is often mocked and beaten, Artyom promises him protection. But this promise proves burdensome to Artyom, who finally decides to go back on his word and leave Cain to his own devices.

The story is remarkable among Gorky's longer tales for its lack of philosophizing. Things simply are as they are: Cain exists to be beaten, and Artyom to oppress others. For a brief moment the natural order of things turns around, and as a result something is not quite right. Artyom remains ill at ease in his role of protector, while Cain has a constant presentiment that something will go wrong. After he decides to abandon Cain, Artyom feels no guilt and peacefully dozes off. The strong feel no pity for the weak in Gorky's world.

"Malva" contains one of Gorky's best early portraits of a female character. In some ways, as was noted by Gorky's contemporaries, Malva resembles other women in Gorky's stories, going back to Izergil.[24] All are independent, strong figures who flout conventional rules of morality in much the same way that Gorky's male vagabonds challenge other social norms. Occasionally Gorky tended to sentimentalize his women characters, especially in his treatment of prostitutes. For instance, "The Woman with Blue Eyes" ("Zhenshchina s golubymi glazami," 1895) is about a widow who maintains her dignity even after she turns to prostitution to support her children; the narrator of "Once in Autumn" ("Odnazhdy osen'iu," 1894) tells how a prostitute helped him find shelter when he was cold and hungry; and a lonely prostitute has a youthful narrator write love letters to and from the imaginary title figure in "Boles" (1896). Malva, though, is far from sentimental. She has had a long-standing affair with Vasily, who lives on a spur of land where he works as a fishery watchman. Yakov, the son Vasily has not seen since leaving home five years before, comes to persuade his father to return. With only minimal effort on her part, Malva causes the son to fall in love with her as well. A violent rivalry arises between father and son. In the end, though, Malva goes off with neither, but with Sergei, a powerful, hard-drinking, insolent fisherman who has had his eye on her all along.

Despite their bitter conflict, Yakov and Vasily are more alike than they realize, and eventually reach a tacit understanding. Yakov cannot comprehend his father's abandonment of the land, but then he himself is all too readily seduced by the freer life along the shore and, of course, by Malva herself. The real gulf, however, lies between Yakov and Vasily on the one hand, and Malva on the other. Both men depend upon Malva for their temporary happiness, but she wants true independence. Her interest in them (and no doubt in Sergei as well) is only temporary. She enjoys a much more profound freedom than either of them will ever attain.

Lost Illusions

Among the stories Gorky wrote in the late 1890s are several in which characters either have ideals that are tarnished or else get a glimpse of a better world that remains beyond their reach. In both cases the result is despair.

"Creatures That Once Were Men" ("Byvshie liudi," 1897; literally "Ex-People") belongs, like Konovalov, to Gorky's Kazan cycle. In a memoir of 1928 Gorky mentions that he first saw the main figure in "Creatures That Once Were Men," Kuvalda, in court, being prosecuted for beating up an innkeeper. Possibly Gorky had this incident in mind when he ended the story with Kuvalda's arrest.

The down-and-outers who inhabit Kuvalda's lodging are influenced by two people. One is Kuvalda himself, a retired army captain of imposing physique and cheerful disposition, but also with a strong inclination to drink that has brought him far down in life. For all his gregariousness and generosity, though, Kuvalda does not help people get back on their feet but encourages them to remain where they are. His major undertaking in the story is to encourage Vavilov, the proprietor of an inn across the street, to bring suit against Petunnikov, owner of the lodging house that Kuvalda runs. Petunnikov is putting up a factory that juts onto land owned by the inn. Vavilov ends up settling with Petunnikov for a trifling sum, but then is forced to give most of the money over to Kuvalda and the other "ex-people" for their help in the suit. Kuvalda fails to stop the factory, though he does get the satisfaction of using the money he obtains to arrange a feast for his fellow creatures.

The other main influence is a man known as the "teacher" because he originally taught. Since then he has worked at other jobs; at the time of the story he is a reporter for a local newspaper. Like Kuvalda, he is well educated and comes from a better background; the two men are in fact friends and drinking companions. The teacher, though, dreams of something better. Although he lacks the will to stop drinking and leave Kuvalda's lodging, he teaches and helps others. The hopeless drunkards at the lodging house are closer to Kuvalda, while those who still have some self-respect are inclined toward the teacher, who writes petitions for his fellow "creatures," publishes notices on their behalf in the paper, and tries to instill in them a degree of pride. At the end of the story, worn out by alcoholism, he is brought back to the lodging mortally ill. He dies as the others carouse on the money they have received from Vavilov's settlement with Petunnikov. The next day, as the teacher's body is taken away, Kuvalda gets into an altercation and is arrested. The "creatures" thus lose both their physical support, Kuvalda, and their spiritual guide, the teacher.

Gorky's masterpiece of the 1890s is a brief tale in which incident, character, and description combine to create a nearly perfect story. "Twenty-Six Men and a Girl" ("Dvadtsat' shest' i odna," 1899) is again set in Kazan. Subtitled "A Poem," it describes the existence of twenty-six men who labor from six in the morning until ten at night working in a damp basement room that houses a bakery. Little brightens their dreary days except for the visits of Tanya, a sixteen-year-old maidservant who works in an embroidery shop on the second floor of the building. When she stops by each morning the men give her pretzels and do various favors for her in the hope that she will continue to visit. Next door to the room where the men make pretzels is another section of the bakery, in which four men prepare rolls under distinctly better working conditions. A new worker in that section, an ex-soldier and something of a dandy, visits the twenty-six men, and on one occasion boasts of his admirers among the women who work upstairs. The baker in the pretzel section claims that their Tanya would be no easy conquest. The ex-soldier promises success within two weeks, a period filled with foreboding for the twenty-six. When Tanya succumbs, the men surround her, shouting angrily at her, for she has taken away their happiness. She contemptuously shouts back, walks through the crowd of men as though they were not there, and never returns.

This work is highly effective for several reasons. One is that it is very tightly constructed. The seduction scene, to take just a single example, is symmetrical: first the twenty-six crowd around, then Tanya is shown going into the cellar, to be followed by the soldier. After the seduction the action is reversed: first the soldier emerges, then Tanya, and finally the men from the bakery crowd around her. Into the middle of all this, as the twenty-six wait, the author inserts an equally symmetrical description of the weather.[25] In Gorky's longer, less intense, and usually less unified stories the descriptions tend to be more leisurely, and acquire power through accumulation. In "Twenty-Six Men and a Girl" the details are spare and the impact sudden. Another factor is the unusually evocative imagery, which in several instances has religious content. The monstrous oven dominating the pretzel bakery resembles a pagan deity, while Tanya herself is depicted as an idol to whom the men make ritual sacrifices.[26] The settings also play a notable role in the narrative. The men's moldy underground chamber is contrasted both to the room in which rolls are produced and to the second floor where Tanya works. When she arrives she stands at the threshold, several steps above where the men work. It is as though others come from a higher and better world unattainable to the twenty-six.

The theme of the story combines a statement on human nature with an insight into the relationship between a group and an individual. As Helen Muchnic has stated succinctly, at its core lies "man's tragic inclination to destroy himself unwittingly by setting traps for what he loves and lives by."[27] The story is unusual because it illustrates this tendency, not through the "I" so pervasive in Gorky's early stories, but through a collective "we": the narrator speaks in the plural and never separates himself from the others. Only the baker who prods the ex-soldier into seducing Tanya is referred to individually several times.[28] His position seems to have made him a de facto leader, and so he becomes the group's voice, articulating a belief in Tanya that they all share.

Another aspect of the theme is perhaps best illustrated by reference to a story that Gorky wrote not long before: "Notch" ("Zazubrina," 1897). The prisoner "Notch" enjoys entertaining his fellow inmates. But he has a rival in a playful kitten, which the prisoners also love. Angry at the tiny scene-stealer, he dips the kitten in green paint, at first to the amusement of the other prisoners. When it becomes clear that the kitten is in pain and about to suffocate, Notch's comrades beat him badly. That he eventually recovers his former position is implied by the last paragraph of the story: "The kitten disappeared from that time on. And Notch no longer had to share the attention of the prison's inhabitants with anybody" (3:172). The group's admiration makes "Notch" a worse person than he would be otherwise.[29]

If we keep "Notch" in mind, the worship of Tanya by the twenty-six men appears in a different light. Granted, she is not cruel, and most commentators on the story have seen her as a positive figure— a person who maintains her independence despite the men's efforts to turn her into an idol. Nevertheless, until she loses her luster at the end she enjoys and even takes advantage of their worship. They give her free pretzels and do small chores for her, but when one of them has the temerity to ask her to mend his only shirt, she refuses with contempt. To them she is an ideal; in reality, she is an ordinary person—and thus her "fall" at the end is nothing unusual. What is more, the workers' interest in Tanya turns them away from their own inner strength. That resource emerges in their singing: all twenty-six sing as a unit, their voices echoing through the shop giving them strength to get through their daily tasks. The true ideal, says Gorky, resides in oneself and in the group to which one belongs; it is futile to seek it in others.

Chapter Three
The Young Novelist
Rebels without a Cause

Gorky's stories may examine a single crucial moment in the lives of his characters ("Chelkash"), or they may deal with a series of incidents ("Konovalov"). In either case they differ from his novels not so much in length—several of his stories are quite long—as in scope. The novels do not concentrate on brief intervals but instead usually detail almost the entire life of the main hero. The first and shorter part of the Gorkian novel comprises a self-contained bildungsroman in which the protagonist learns about the surrounding world and seeks to define his relationship with other individuals and with society at large. Once the person reaches young adulthood the work becomes more of a sociological or sociopolitical novel. Through his main figure Gorky exposes what he sees as the evils of bourgeois society, most often concentrating on the merchant class and the emerging industrialists who were beginning to dominate Russia's economic life. The work concludes with the physical or at least the spiritual death of the hero. Not every novel follows this formula precisely, and the most famous, *Mother,* does not do so at all. Still, Gorky's novels generally fit this pattern, both the prerevolutionary works discussed here and the two later works treated in Chapter Six.

By the time Gorky's first acknowledged novel, *Foma Gordeev* (1899), appeared, he was already an established short story writer. The novel reveals a mature talent, and its title character has been frequently cited as perhaps the most successful protagonist of Gorky's longer works.[1] In addition, *Foma Gordeev* has numerous primary and secondary characters in a wide range of settings with nicely interwoven conflicts.

The novel begins, not with Foma himself, but with two representatives of the older generation: Ignat Gordeev, Foma's father; and Yakov Mayakin, Ignat's friend and Foma's godfather. Ignat is the precursor of the strong, somewhat crude, but essentially good entrepreneurs who appear in some of the plays Gorky wrote during the 1910s, for instance Antipa Zykov in *The Zykovs* and Ivan Mastakov in *The Old Man*. Gorky admired the self-made men who emerged from Russia's peasantry, viewing them as people of talent and determination who possessed the ability not just to accumulate wealth but also to improve the lot of others.[2] Ignat Gordeev at first worked on a river barge belonging to a wealthy merchant; by the age of forty he already owned three steamships and ten barges on the Volga. As Gorky describes him, Ignat is motivated partly by greed, but also by his unlimited energy. Recognizing no obstacles, he heads directly toward his goal. Though his strength and spontaneity drive him to ride roughshod over others, they also make him straightforward and generous. There is something invigorating about these new millionaires, not yet tamed by the mores of refined society.

Ignat's longtime acquaintance, Yakov Mayakin, is an entirely different sort. Yakov comes from an old merchant family, which dates back at least to the time of Catherine the Great. Well respected among other merchants, intelligent, and cunning, he does not share Ignat's natural openness: "His high, wrinkled forehead blended into his bald spot, and it seemed that this person had two faces: the one that everyone could see was penetrating and intelligent, with a long, cartiliginous nose; the other had no eyes, only wrinkles, behind which Mayakin seemed to be hiding both his eyes and lips, hiding them until the right moment, and when it would come Mayakin would look at the world with different eyes and smile with a different smile" (4:195). Religion plays a large role in the Mayakin family life; the day begins and ends with prayers, and Yakov's favorite reading is the Book of Job. The spirit of the household precludes fairy tales, and the young Foma Gordeev, brought there as an infant to be raised after his mother dies in childbirth, hears such tales only later, from his aunt Anfisa, after Ignat has brought him back to his own house.

Foma Gordeev largely involves the history of the two families, as well as the changes that occur between one generation and the next. The chronicle of the Gordeev family as it unfolds in the novel recalls those of families that Gorky decribed in such other works as his late novel *The Artamonov Business* and his autobiographical *Childhood*. The family fortune is founded by a powerful, shrewd individual, but the next generation lacks the ability, the will, perhaps even the desire to maintain the business. Both the enterprise and the family itself enter upon a decline from which they cannot recover. Gorky was not the only Russian writer of his time to explore such phenomena within families. Chekhov treats the merchant class in "Three Years"[3] and deals with the decline of village shopowners in "In the Ravine," while Bunin treats the waning of gentry families in "Sukhodol."[4] Gorky's works differ from these by the heroic dimensions he bestows upon the founders of these short-lived dynasties.

The Mayakin family, in contrast, to the Gordeevs, is less spectacular, but it endures. Yakov's son Taras has left the family and been disowned by the father for marrying against his wishes. Rumor reports that Taras has been in trouble with the authorities; the reader half expects that he has become a revolutionary. But when the prodigal son returns toward the end of the novel, he has evolved into an even more successful and ruthless businessman than his father. Yakov's daughter Lyuba, who as an adolescent is attracted to books and develops a social consciousness, later returns to the fold as well, and eventually marries a young industrialist. The "hereditary" merchants go on as before.

Both Ignat and Yakov have become urban merchants; Anany Shchurov, who appears in the novel only briefly, is a lumber merchant from the country. While Ignat Gordeev has been in small part polished by the city, Shchurov retains all the rough edges and native slyness of a self-made robber baron. Contradictions swirl about him. Despite wild rumors of his cruelty and debauchery, he talks nobly of the need for work and complains that machinery has deprived people of their freedom. In one and the same breath he talks of God's mercy and haggles over money with a determination that matches Mayakin's. His physical apearance is as Janus-like as his personality: his calm eyes make the upper part of his face seem wisely virtuous, but his thick, red lips do not seem to belong to the same person.[5] In origin more like Ignat, he operates with Yakov's tenacious prudence. When he bests Foma during a meeting between the two, it becomes clear just how ill equipped the younger Gordeev is to cope with the milieu in which he has been raised.

Like most of Gorky's early works, *Foma Gordeev* underwent many revisions even after publication. Gorky abbreviated descriptions, eliminated superfluous adjectives and adverbs, made the vocabulary more precise, and in general tightened up the writing.[6] He also paid a great deal of attention to the speech of his merchants, especially to Yakov's. He and Ignat, like other people of their class, use an old-fashioned language filled with folk sayings and proverbs.[7] In this novel, perhaps more than in any other, Gorky differentiates his characters by their manner of speaking, and nowhere are those distinctions so clear as for his merchants.

Foma Gordeev stands not so much opposed to as apart from the merchant class to which he supposedly belongs, and that is his tragedy. Opposition would at least imply a direction to his life, but that is what he lacks. In reworking his novel Gorky was careful to eliminate references to other paths that Foma might have followed— such as becoming a vagabond or a religious pilgrim.[8] His only option is to drift aimlessly; whenever he acts on his own volition he does so more out of impulse than out of forethought.

Foma possesses neither the determination of his father nor the cunning business sense of Mayakin, who for a long time seems to be grooming Foma to replace his missing son. The task of turning Foma into a merchant is too much even for Mayakin, and he quickly gives up on him once Taras returns. At the end of the novel Foma appears at a party to dedicate a new steamer recently purchased by one of the merchants. Having drunk heavily, he begins to berate the merchants by name for their transgressions. A fight ensues, and Foma is overpowered. Sent off to a hospital, he returns to the town three years later and wanders about half-crazed and nearly always drunk—an object more of scorn than of pity.

Foma Gordeev—his surname, ironically, means "proud"—recognizes the corruption and hollowness of the merchant class from his position within it. Ilya Lunev, the main charcter in *The Three of Them* (*Troe,* 1901), strives to enter that class; only once inside does he become fully aware of the qualities that repel Foma.[9] Lunev—the name refers to a type of hawk, a bird of prey—resembles Foma in his background. Both are shunted about as children, both get along more easily with prostitutes than with other women, both are profoundly unhappy without knowing quite why, both turn a celebratory occasion into a scandalous outburst against bourgeois society, and both are destroyed. The differences between them, however, are more fundamental than the resemblances. Not only are they born into different classes, but Lunev possesses an ambition absent in Gordeev. In his moving from country to the city, in attempting to cast off his peasant heritage and become a merchant, he more nearly recalls Foma's father Ignat.[10] The differences between the protagonists affect the novels: *Foma Gordeev,* though a powerful portrayal of the merchant class, seems narrower, more static; *The Three of Them,* in showing that the effort to move into that society exacts a fearful spiritual price, offers a broader, if at times more diffuse picture.

The title refers to a group of boyhood acquintances, each of whom follows a different path in life. Here again Gorky singles out one character as the linchpin of his novel, though this time the other two figures play fairly important roles. Yakov Filimonov is the son of a bartender at an inn, a distant relative of the Lunevs who takes in Ilya and his uncle. Maltreated by his father, Yakov attempts to escape through his reading. He and Masha, the even more delicate daughter of a cobbler who lives in the same house, devour books about knights and princes who overcome evil intrigues and live happily ever after. Escapism, though, helps little in real life. Even as Yakov grows into adulthood he suffers brutal beatings from his father whenever he shows the slightest sign of independence. At the end, dying from tuberculosis, he still reads his adventure stories, expressing no desire for a different life or any bitterness toward those who have harmed him.

Pavel Grachev is a very different sort. Left to fend for himself when his father is imprisoned for killing his mother in a fit of jealousy, Pavel is apprenticed off to Masha's father. He dislikes the shoemaker's trade and soon runs away. Although he comes back after a while, he turns out to have the soul of a vagabond. Of the novel's major figures only he both rejects society's values and has the strength to strike out on an independent path. He also turns into a budding poet. The excerpts from his verses provide evidence of his growth from despair over his harsh life, to a greater reflectiveness, and finally to a certain optimism in a poem he publishes in a newspaper.[11] Yet Pavel resembles Ezhov in his failure to transform his good intentions into action. In a scene that may well mirror the opening scenes of Tolstoy's novel, *Resurrection,* Pavel visits the place where his former lover, a prostitute named Vera, is being tried for robbery. When she confesses her guilt and faces a certain prison sentence, Pavel can only watch helplessly. Though more positive than either of the other members of his trio, he is not at all an ideal figure.

Ilya Lunev, unlike Pavel and Yakov, can cope with his barbarous surroundings. Neither a victim like Yakov nor a renegade like Pavel,

Ilya for a while manages to get ahead in life. Beginning as a helper to a ragman, "Granddad" Eremei, he then becomes an apprentice and a peddler who hopes to start his own business. Through Pavel and Vera he meets Olimpiada, another of the prostitutes so frequently encountered in these early novels. She is planning to marry an old moneychanger in exchange for a tidy sum. One day, having wandered into the moneychanger's shop, Ilya more or less spontaneously kills him and takes some of the money that is lying about. He is suspected to a degree, and on several occasions is on the verge of confessing, but the police are never seriously on his trail. He rents a room from a young middle-class couple, Tatyana and Kirik Avtonomov, who eventually offer to help him finance his own shop. Externally, his life goes well, though internally he burns with a hidden anger. Attending Vera's trial finally causes Ilya to go over the edge: at a party for Tatyana that same evening he reveals to all the guests that he has had an affair with Tatyana and that he killed the moneychanger. As the police are taking him to jail, he breaks away and kills himself by running at full speed headfirst into a wall.

As with Foma Gordeev, part of Ilya's problem is illustrated by his attitudes toward women. He too prefers brief encounters with streetwalkers to a more enduring love. His one serious romance, with Olimpiada, is doomed to failure from the start: he is too jealous and too naive to be a suitable partner for her. In his affair with Tatyana she is the aggressor rather then he. The one woman who might have helped Ilya is Sofia Medvedeva, a young socialist who challenges his whole way of life. But Ilya does not wish to change, and soon quarrels with her. His falling into destructive relationships and turning away from those who could help him are symptomatic of a larger problem. Like Foma Gordeev before him, Lunev cannot forge links with others. He remains imprisoned by a combination of pride and confusion, the legacy of a broken childhood.

Revolution

The events of 1905, in which Gorky was a direct participant and which led to his exile from Russia for some eight years, had a great impact on his subsequent writing. His next two novels reflected the spirit of those times, though from opposite standpoints. Thus *Mother* (*Mat'*, 1906–7), because of its depiction of the modern revolutionary as well as its wholehearted commitment to the cause of social change, has come to be considered the founding work of socialist realism. *The Life of a Useless Man (Zhizn' nenuzhnogo cheloveka,* 1907) views events from the other side, through the eyes of a police spy, within whom revolutionary forces inspire fear and awe. *Mother,* perhaps Gorky's most revolutionary work, turns out to be an anomaly among his novels in its characters and its structure, while Gorky's story about a police agent is centered on a figure who bears a strong resemblance to the heroes of his first novels.

Gorky wrote the greater part of *Mother* during his troubled visit of 1906 to the United States, and the book's first publication was in English, in an American edition of 1907. That early version remains even now the one most familiar to American audiences. Gorky, however, significantly revised the book on two occasions. His final text is shorter, without some of the excesses that mar the original manuscript. He makes his points more concisely, with less pathos; for instance, the mother's speech to the crowd when she is arrested at the end of the novel is shortened, and the entire court scene is made less heavy-handed. Some minor characters who appear only fleetingly in the original version are eliminated, along with some of the author's lyrical digressions. Two of the more important secondary characters—the anarchist Mikhail Rybin and the son's close acquaintance, Andrei Nakhodka—express their views somewhat less vehemently. The mother's evolution from total noncomprehension to absolute commitment is smoother and more direct. The references to religion, while still important, are less prominent. [12]

The main events in *Mother* had been on Gorky's mind for some time before he wrote the novel. In 1902 a large May Day demonstration took place at Sormovo, a shipbuilding complex near Nizhny Novgorod. Among its leaders was Pyotr Zalomov, who became the model for the son, Pavel Vlasov. Pyotr's mother, Anna Zalomova, a distant relative of Gorky's, had visited his home when he was a child. Her husband, a factory worker, drank heavily and died relatively young, leaving her with seven children to raise. Like the character for whom she is the model, Pelageya Nilovna Vlasova (addressed as Nilovna throughout the novel), Anna Zalomova followed her son into revolutionary activity. [13]

The influence of these and numerous other real-life prototypes may have been responsible for making *Mother* even more descriptive and less oriented toward plot than usual. The opening chapters describe Pavel's background and his early revolutionary work. After

Pavel's first arrest, Nilovna gradually becomes drawn into political activism, which culminates, at the end of part 1, in the scene based on the demonstration at Sormovo. Pavel, who had been released, is again arrested, as are others among the revolutionaries. While Pavel languishes in jail, Nilovna continues her underground work for the cause. The key occurrence of the second part is Pavel's trial, at which the defendants make stirring speeches on their own behalf. The book ends with the mother's arrest as she distributes copies of her son's speech at a train station. Overall the book resembles a set of "scenes from revolutionary life" more than a typical novel; there is little intrigue among the characters, and except for Nilovna herself the most important figures from part 1 are largely absent from part 2.

Even though the doctrine of socialist realism was promulgated in the early 1930s, more than twenty-five years after *Mother* was written, the novel had great influence on party theoreticians. What qualities made *Mother* so exemplary? Rufus Mathewson has singled out two notable "formulas" clearly expressed in *Mother* that recur in much Soviet fiction: the "conversion of the innocent" (that is, Nilovna) into an active revolutionary, and a "pattern of emblematic political heroism in the face of terrible obstacles" (Pavel).[14] One may generalize from Mathewson's comments; not only these two figures, but many of the secondary characters as well, represent types of revolutionary activists found in much Soviet fiction.[15] Mathewson is right, though, in emphasizing the importance of the mother and son, who stand out as Gorky's main models. Neither deviates from the chosen path. Nilovna passes without hesitation from political ignorance to revolutionary devotion, while Pavel can be fanatical in his absolute adherence to the cause. They are distant indeed from the alienated protagonists of Gorky's previous novels. Gorky creates revolutionary archetypes: the son stands for the whole younger generation of revolutionaries, while the mother represents an older generation that coalesces with its offspring. *Mother* embodies what might be termed a myth of the revolutionary spirit.[16]

Although not everyone approved of Gorky's decision to focus on the mother, that approach does add two dimensions to the novel. The more obvious one is that it allows *Mother* to depict the development of a revolutionary consciousness. Even if the heroine is motivated by a mother's love for her son, Gorky still illustrates how a person totally alien to politics can be swept up by the movement. Less obvious, but just as important, is the fact that Gorky justifies the workers' cause by showing it through Nilovna's eyes. At first, her very lack of comprehension creates an effect of "estrangement": the actions appear strange to her since she is experiencing them for the first time and lacks any context in which to place them. As her comprehension increases, Nilovna overcomes her fear and begins to accept the revolutionaries' reasons for resorting to violence.[17] The uninitiated reader, carried along step by step as Nilovna's acceptance of the workers' program grows, is more likely to be convinced by her than by Pavel, whose appeal is largely limited to those already fully committed to the revolutionary cause.

The one element of the novel that accords least with its status as a paragon of socialist realism is its religion. Even Pavel in his early days hangs on his wall a picture of Christ after the resurrection— albeit later he does question organized religion. The anarchist Mikhail Rybin tells Pavel that "it is necessary to invent a new faith . . . to create a God who is a friend of the people!" (8:57). Here Rybin approaches the "God-building" doctrine that Gorky espoused a short while later in *A Confession*. Andrei Nakhodka is one of the novel's more complex figures; unlike Pavel, he wonders about committing violence in the name of the cause, and on more than one occasion expresses thoughts about God not dissimilar to Rybin's. No character ruminates more on religion than Nilovna herself, a devout believer whose faith is shaken by the new ideas to which she has been exposed. She continues to believe and eventually feels closer to Christ, but she grows hostile to a church that seems to have moved away from Christ's teachings. Nilovna's statements about religion in the final version are less extensive than they were in the original English publication,[18] and yet enough remains to indicate that Gorky attacks religion, specifically the Russian Orthodox Church, for many of the same reasons that motivate his criticism of the middle class. Both support the status quo, ignore poverty, and are hypocritical in their profession of good intentions. Religious feeling, which Gorky seeks to rescue from the church and return to the people, is to be centered on Christ as understood by Pavel and Nilovna, or on the "new God" that Nakhodka and Rybin mention. The spiritual concerns in *Mother*, sometimes ignored or belittled by modern critics, are in fact integral to Gorky's depiction of the workers' movement, and also an index of his own thinking at the time.

Gorky's next novel, the first he wrote entirely on Capri, offered a totally different view of Russia's growing revolutionary movement. *The Life of a Useless Man*—at first called *The Spy (Shpion)* and originally translated into English under that title—comprises the biography of Evsei Klimkov, a police spy. In many ways the novel's structure parallels that of Gorky's earlier novels. Once again the hero loses his parents at a young age, and the first chapters detail the early development of his personality. The rest of the novel broadens in scope to treat Russia's social ills: the women characters are often prostitutes, while the men are greedy, unprincipled individuals seeking their own advantage.

What makes the novel unique for Gorky is the specific group of men with which it deals: the network of police spies in a provincial town. With one or two exceptions the spies are without redeeming qualities; they tend to be as unattractive physically as they are morally. Over the last half of the novel loom the events of 1905, which stir unrest even in the provinces and cause panic among the spies, who feel hunted. The central character is also new for Gorky. Though neither Foma Gordeev nor Ilya Lunev could be called heroic, both display a potential that is defeated by their environment. Evsei, on the other hand, is a lost soul from the start. As a boy he was a bad pupil because he was constantly afraid the other students would beat him or wrong him in some way. He liked church, not from any religious feeling but because it was cozy and quiet there; people were well behaved, with none of the brawling that frightened him outside. Later, when he has already worked as a spy, he wishes he could retreat to a monastery, again not for the sake of faith but out of a desire to escape from the rest of the world (9:93). At the end, disgusted by his surviving colleagues and too indecisive to break with them in any other way, he throws himself under a train. Even then he almost changes his mind at the last minute.

Gorky's interest in revolutionary activity sustains a third relatively obscure novel of the period, *A Summer (Leto,* 1909). If *Mother* depicts the period preceding the 1905 revolution, and *The Life of a Useless Man* presents, if only as an echo, the revolutionary upheavals of that fateful year, then *A Summer* describes their aftermath. Also, while the first two works primarily show the workers' movement within an urban setting, *A Summer* examines the growth of political awareness among the peasantry.

A Summer displays the strong influence of the two preceding novels, and in particular that of *Mother*. Indeed, along with a diary that Gorky received from a peasant involved in revolutionary work, a planned but unwritten sequel to *Mother* provided the main source for *A Summer*. [19] In his anarchistic rebellion the former soldier Mikhail Gnedoy recalls Mikhail Rybin from *Mother*. Egor Dosekin, the peasant who expresses revolutionary ideals most convincingly, recalls Pavel Vlasov in his outlook if not his background. He even speaks differently than the other peasants in the novel: while his vocabulary is typical for a person of his background, his speeches are more concise and better reasoned than those of his comrades. [20] Also, the novel resembles *Mother* in its general presentation of an awakening consciousness within previously ignorant people, in its depiction of the seemingly inexorable growth of the revolutionary movement, and in the nature of its ending, which in one sense is a defeat (the arrest of Gnedoy and the narrator) but also contains the seeds of future victories (the two conduct revolutionary propaganda among the soldiers guarding them).

There are noteworthy similarities between *A Summer* and *Confession*, which Gorky had completed just before commencing work on it. [21] For example, *A Summer* is also told in the first person, though it deals only with the events of a single summer. More significantly, at least two figures could have come from the earlier novel. One is Pyotr Kuzin, an older peasant and the firmest religious believer in the novel. Formerly a dogmatic follower of Russian Orthodoxy, he becomes sympathetic to the goals of the revolutionaries but interprets them in his own way, which resembles God-building. The novel's narrator, Egor Trofimov, is a less religious version of Matvei, the narrator of *A Confession*. Trofimov is a revolutionary more by instinct than by conviction. Like Matvei he is a wanderer, a pilgrim in search of the "truth." Sensitive both to nature and to his fellows, he is still groping for definite answers of the sort others have found. By making him the central character Gorky shows that the concerns expressed in *A Confession* had not disappeared overnight. Granted, *A Summer* is definitely a revolutionary novel; in its more modest way it is as one-sided in its presentation of the issues as *Mother*. And yet Gorky still sought to combine revolution with religion, an ambition that had received its fullest expression just a year before.

A Confession

Perhaps none of Gorky's novels received so much contemporary attention as *A Confession* (*Ispoved'*, 1908). The reason for the interest is simple enough: in this novel Gorky seemingly adopted positions diametrically opposed to those he had taken in his previous works. From politically charged novels such as *Mother* and *The Life of a Useless Man* Gorky had made an about-face to write a novel about a religious seeker. What is more, his protagonist finds the truth he has sought in "God-building," the "religious Marxism" being set forth at about this time in works by Gorky, Alexander Bogdanov, and Anatoly Lunacharsky. More orthodox Marxists—Georgy Plekhanov, Vatslav Vorovsky, and Lenin himself—had little good to say of Gorky's book; on the other hand, such Russian symbolists as Andrei Bely, Alexander Blok, and Georgy Chulkov, who had frequently criticized Gorky in the past, suddenly found *A Confession* a work they could praise enthusiastically.[22]

Structurally, the novel contains little that is new for Gorky, with the one major exception of its first-person narration. Since Matvei tells his own story directly, Gorky indulges in fewer of the authorial digressions that tend to slow his novels down. The scenes become more immediate and more striking. Matvei's pronouncements are not always totally convincing: in particular, Gorky should have had him describe his youthful religious feelings in more detail, for his faith is more asserted than shown. Still, the experiment with the first-person technique prepares the way for the highly effective narrative in Gorky's autobiographical writings and memoirs of a few years later.

Gorky's contemporary critics, however, were more concerned with his God-building. In Gorky's stories of the 1890s, as well as in his early novels and plays, many of the characters had expressed an interest in religion, but questions of faith were generally not prominent. But in *A Confession* Matvei travels about as a kind of spiritual pilgrim, many of the other characters display at least an outward concern with religion, and much of the novel is set in monasteries and convents. This departure for Gorky is not so great as it might at first appear, for the ideas put forth in *A Confession* were formulated in embryonic form by Rybin, Nakhodka, and Nilovna in *Mother*. Evsei Klimkov, Gorky's "useless man," lacks Matvei's religious sensibility but considers starting a new life by going off to a monastery. In the two preceding novels, though, Gorky had paid much attention to political matters, such as the organization of workers' movements and the conflicts between the authorities and revolutionaries. In *A Confession* he emphasizes internal qualities, the spiritual crises of Matvei and other individuals.

A foundling raised by a church sexton named Larion, Matvei devotes his life to discovering, in Tolstoy's words, "what men live by." He enjoys a blissful childhood under the benevolent guidance of Larion and his friend Savelka Migun. To the outside world Savelka seems a drunkard and a thief, but he is redeemed by his wonderful singing and telling of folk tales. For his part, Larion speaks with compassion about Christ, displays a deep love for people in general, and has a special rapport with animals. But Larion accidentally drowns. Subsequently taken in by the steward of an estate, Matvei is introduced to the world of money and ambition. His sense of innocence and beauty gradually fades. Marriage to the steward's daughter briefly restores his happiness, but after their first child is born his wife becomes engrossed in material matters. She soon dies in childbirth, and when his firstborn dies as well, Matvei begins his wanderings.

Although Marxist critics disliked the novel, its scenes of organized religion present such an unflattering picture of Russian Orthodoxy that church officials asked to have it banned.[23] Matvei's travels take him to various monasteries, which are run as though they were businesses, with shrines drawing in pilgrims and worshipers. His entering a monastery as a novice only leads to total disillusionment: individual monks are greedy, domineering, and hypocritical. One of the people to whom Matvei is briefly drawn, Father Antony, is a well-off gentleman who has bought his way into the monastery. His life there, however, is at least as debauched as it was before. Perhaps it is too much to identify Antony with Tolstoy,[24] but certainly the almost hypnotic power he has over Matvei, his seeming to toy with Matvei's beliefs, and a certain crudeness in his behavior are all qualities that appear as well in Gorky's subsequent memoir of Tolstoy.

The Okurov Cycle

Immediately after *A Confession* appeared Gorky deemphasized his spiritual interests to explore social and political issues within a more conventional framework. The Okurov "cycle" consists of two completed works: *The Town of Okurov* (*Gorodok Okurov*, 1909), a relatively short work, and *The Life of Matvei Kozhemiakin (Zhizn' Matveia Ko-zhemiakina,* 1910–11), which, except for Gorky's massive and never completed *Life of Klim Samgin,* was his longest novel. The lopsided nature of the cycle derived from Gorky's changing conceptions as he wrote rapidly during his productive middle years on Capri. At the start he planned a large novel in three parts. After completing *The Town of Okurov* he set to work on the intended third part, *A Great Love (Bol'shaia liubov'),* but soon put it aside and never returned to it (the surviving remnant can be found in 10:633–60). Lyubov Matushkina, who was to be the main character of *A Great Love,* did play a prominent role in the final pages of the second part, *The Life of Matvei Kozhemiakin.* Perhaps Gorky was then planning to return to the third part and carry her story forward, but he did not do so.

For some time Gorky apparently regarded *The Town of Okurov* as the title of the entire trilogy; the first section of *The Life of Matvei Kozhemiakin* was published as though it were simply a continuation of *The Town of Okurov.* Only later did Gorky come to see the two parts of the cycle as independent works. And indeed they are quite different. While the setting and some of the characters are the same, and though the works overlap chronologically, they diverge markedly in scope, theme, and narrative manner.[25] They form a cycle chiefly because they offer complementary views of both the town and of what has come to be known as "Okurovism."

Gorky subtitled *The Town of Okurov* "A Chronicle." While that term would be accurate for *The Life of Matvei Kozhemiakin,* the first part of the cycle is more a glimpse of Russian provincial life specifically in 1904–5, the period of Russia's first revolutionary outbreaks. More than the second part of the cycle, *The Town of Okurov* contains detailed physical descriptions of both the town and its environs. The Putanitsa River divides the town into two districts: Shikhan, where the better people live, and Zarechie, home to those lower in the social order. Okurov is not impoverished—indeed, the merchants at least are quite well off, and many live in fine houses—but life there is oppressive. It is a kind of Russian "everytown." The disease that infects such towns, "Okurovism," represents not just backwardness and provincialism, but also the social forces that drag everybody down to a common level.

The events of 1905 reach Okurov only as a vague echo, but they profoundly affect the lives of the four people through whom Gorky shows the town's more unattractive aspects. Significantly, all come from the poorer Zarechie district. Somewhat to one side of the other three stands Tyunov, who has wandered about far from Okurov for long periods of time, has lost an eye as the result of his adventures, and in both parts of the cycle speaks of what he sees as the responsibilities and the failures of the merchant class. While he lacks the religious dimension of Matvei in *A Confession* or Luka in *The Lower Depths,* he is nonetheless one of Gorky's seekers of truth.[26] He wants people to think about why they were put on earth.

At one point Tyunov refers to the writings of Kozhemiakin (who plays a very minor role in *The Town of Okurov*): "I met an old man, he's writing a history for us and has been writing it for thirteen years. He's already covered about twenty pounds of paper, to judge by the looks of it" (10:30). Kozhemiakin, according to Tyunov, has said he is trying to depict the sad existence of the petty bourgeoisie in Russia, and to be sure the other major characters in the story show that Okurov offers Kozhemiakin an endless amount of material. Vavilo Burmistrov lives only to fight and cause trouble, yet his very disruptiveness marks the first step toward revolutionary upheaval. Sima Devushkin, a young poet, lacks Vavilo's strength. His poetry expresses resignation and defeat; he finds hope only in his religious beliefs. Vavilo loves the fourth of the key characters, Glafira (nicknamed Lodka); when he finds her and Devushkin together, he kills the poet. The town merchants use the willing Burmistrov as evidence of the disaster that would result from granting people the freedoms for which they have been agitating. But, instead of granting him liberty in return for his cooperation, the town's leading citizens return him to prison. As the novel ends, he is cruelly beaten for resisting. An unrelievedly gloomy picture of Okurov emerges. Vavilo, handsome and powerful, lacks any direction for his anarchistic rebellion. Equally unbound by convention and equally attractive physically, Glafira also gets nowhere with her life. Sima is weakly despairing from the start, while Tyunov's words change little.

In attempting to suggest the nature of his heroes, Gorky makes uncharacteristically frequent use of significant last names. A *burmistr* is a bailiff; the word *tiun* was used in medieval times to denote people bearing roughly the same responsibilities as a nineteenth-century bailiff. Tyunov thus has the more ancient title, but both names refer to people in authority. Their absence of real power underlines the concentration of authority in the hands of the town's "respected" citizens. Devushkin, the surname of the delicate poet, derives from the Russian word for girl. Even the name Kozhemiakin, based on an old word for a leather currier, conveys Matvei's merchant-class origins. They and other characters are both defined and to a degree circumscribed by their appelations.

When Gorky began the second part of the cycle, his first impulse was to "open up" the work, to use the chronicle kept by Matvei Kozhemiakin as a means of expanding his portrayal. But he focused less on the chronicle than on the chronicler. *The Life of Matvei Kozhemiakin* at first glance resembles *Foma Gordeev* and *The Three of Them*. The first section describes the hero's boyhood and youth; the other three sections focus on distinct stages of his adult life. Once again a domineering father, Savely Kozhemiakin, gives way to a weaker, or at least less decisive, son, Matvei. The protagonist's flaws again derive in part from childhood traumas: Gorky's central characters almost never know both natural parents. Here Matvei's mother leaves home when he is a child and remains only a vague memory for him. And, as in most of the novels, the hero's life is described from beginning to end.

Yet there are significant differences between this novel and the preceding work, differences that can largely be traced back to the use of the word *chronicle* to describe the cycle's first part. While Kozhemiakin witnesses all the events in the novel, after the first section it expands to depict not just one person's evolution but also the currents passing through Russian life in general. The reader perceives events of wide significance through the sensibility of a relatively uncultured provincial merchant. In its scope *The Life of Matvei Kozhemiakin* resembles more closely *The Life of Klim Samgin,* albeit Gorky's postrevolutionary epic was a far more ambitious endeavor to create virtually an encyclopedia of Russian life during the decades before 1917. The chroniclelike account, emphasizing important moments rather than individual lives, introduces an almost entirely new set of characters in each of its four sections, so that the novel exhibits even less continuity than is typical for Gorky. The narrative also makes interesting use of Kozhemiakin's writing: particularly in the second section, but to some degree elsewhere as well, large sections of his notebooks are presented. At irregular intervals the text shifts between third-person narration and Matvei's eyewitness accounts. As description and random incidents replace the tense action of the early pages, the text exhibits an unhurried calm. Frequent digressions deepen our understanding of Okurovism, even if they do not always move events forward. Gorky has indeed created a chronicle or sequence of events that seem all the truer for the very lack of dramatic links among them.

Several vivid individuals appear in the first section. Matvei's father, Savely, enters Gorky's pantheon of powerful, domineering merchants. Occasionally warm toward his son, he inspires love, but also fear and a sense of oppression. After his wife runs off to a convent, Savely tells Matvei that she was weak and easily frightened. Thus Matvei's two hereditary lines are defined: part of his character comes from a crude but strong merchant, part from a meek creature who would withdraw from the world. The young boy is also affected by Pushkar, an ex-soldier who works for Savely, and by the deacon Korenev, who gives Matvei formal schooling until the townsfolk insist that Korenev be sent away because of his debauchery and drunkenness.

The heart of the first section consists of a triangle among Savely, his second wife Palaga, and Matvei. Married off in an ill-omened ceremony, Palaga, who is only a few years older than her stepson, cowers before Savely. She and the fifteen-year-old Matvei begin an affair while Savely is away on a trip. Upon his return he learns of what has happened: he beats Palaga but suffers a stroke before he can vent his wrath on Matvei. Savely dies a few days later, followed shortly by Palaga, who succumbs to the injuries inflicted by the beating. Matvei buries her at some distance from his father's grave and plants five birch trees around her resting place; much later, just before his own death, he recalls planting those trees as the one good deed in his life. The section ends with the death of Pushkar, who is buried beside Palaga. Thus almost all the important people from Matvei's formative years have died or disappeared. The only person left is Shakir, a Tatar who came to work for Matvei after Savely's death and remains his loyal companion for the rest of his life.

Three of the novel's key motifs are established in the opening section. First, Matvei, who begins keeping a journal at age thirteen, gathers his random impressions of Okurov and its inhabitants, whose lives center on idle talk and cruelty: for example, he describes several workmen who kill a stray dog by throwing it into a vat of boiling lime. Matvei wants to understand the idle boredom and the barbarity of these people, and yet that comprehension eludes him. Second, organized religion, as in *A Confession,* appears in a bad light. Neither the departure of Matvei's mother for a convent nor Matvei's own stay in a monastery later in the novel is treated positively. Now the way to salvation is political rather than spiritual. Even the best of the religious individuals—Korenev, or the priest Alexander—are portrayed ambiguously. Third, Matvei's lack of ties to any other person or group emerges. From the start he is a black sheep among the town's more prominent individuals; others, aware of his dissatisfaction, respond either by ignoring him or by expressing their dislike directly.[27] His isolation makes him ever less capable of action. Like many of Gorky's characters, he longs for change but is too passive to help bring it about. In this regard Matvei resembles his great literary forebear, Oblomov. While less lazy and fearful than he, Matvei cannot implement his grandiose plans either. He remains an observer, not a doer.[28]

Little is said about happenings in Russia during the 1860s, roughly the era when the action in the first part takes place. But subsequently Kozhemiakin encounters movements and ideas that have penetrated Okurov from the outside. The second section takes place in the mid-1880s. A young widow, Evgenia Mansurova, previously exiled to Siberia for political activity, arrives in Okurov with her young son and becomes a lodger in Kozhemiakin's house. As a populist— one of those who during the previous decade had placed great faith in the peasantry as the wave of Russia's future—Mansurova is taken aback by her conversations with Markusha, the yard porter, who captivates his fellow peasants with folk tales but cynically admits he does not believe anything he says. Although her populist ideals are shaken, Mansurova nonetheless remains committed to an activism that Kozhemiakin both admires and fears. Upon leaving Okurov she also departs from Matvei's life forever, though he never ceases to think about her.

Matvei's aborted relationships are characteristic of the failures he experiences in every aspect of his life. The third section, like the first, contains a triangle; as if to symbolize the decline in his status, this time he is bested by his new yard porter, Maxim, in a rivalry over a seamstress, Goryushina. Maxim and Goryushina are members of a circle led by "Uncle" Mark, another exile returning from Siberia who lives with Kozhemiakin. Of all the characters in the novel, Mark comes closest to serving as Gorky's voice. He wants people to find inspiration in their work and to struggle to make life better. While Kozhemiakin deeply respects Mark, he never quite becomes a regular member of the circle, just as his relationship with Goryushina never quite develops. She and Maxim grow under Mark's influence, while Matvei remains a passive chronicler. The final section of the novel leads up to the events of 1905. Tyunov appears prominently at this point, again expounding on the duties and failures of the merchant class, but not sympathetic either toward the revolutionary forces in society. Now Kozhemiakin ventures into the world, taking up with a married woman. But the affair turns out to be a sham: the husband of the woman he sees encourages the relationship as a means of getting money out of Kozhemiakin. When the scheme fails, the husband kills his wife and then himself. The younger generation comes to the fore: prominent among them are Lyuba Matushkina, daughter of an official and one of the few people to befriend Matvei, and Pyotr Posulov, son of the woman with whom Matvei had his affair. More politically astute and more idealistic than their parents, these young people represent an activism and commitment that Kozhemiakin envies but still does not possess as his life draws to an end.

The Life of Matvei Kozhemiakin is both the longest and the least conventional of Gorky's prerevolutionary novels. It lacks a single story line, and the cast of characters changes drastically from one section to the next. Its interest lies not in intrigue but in the vast panorama of Russian provincial life over a period of several decades that it offers. Theme, not plot, unifies the chronicle; its disparate incidents and characters serve to illustrate the grayness and cruelty of Okurovism. From the narrative manner of this unusual novel it is but a step to Gorky's remarkable autobiographical trilogy, perhaps his finest literary achievement.

Chapter Four

The Plays: A Search for New Forms

The Legacy of Chekhov

When, late in the year 1900, Gorky began to write plays, the leading dramatist in Russia was Anton Chekhov, with whom Gorky had been corresponding since the first edition of his collected works appeared some two years before. At the time Gorky was already well established, having achieved renown with his stories and his first major novel, *Foma Gordeev*. He was completing his next novel, *The Three of Them,* as he began serious work on his plays, apparently seeking new outlets for his talent.

On a number of occasions Gorky had expressed great admiration for both *The Seagull* and *Uncle Vanya,* successfully staged at the Moscow Art Theater in 1898 and 1899 respectively.[1] Chekhov, for his part, encouraged Gorky in his dramatic experiments; in particular he supported the younger writer when he had difficulty completing his first play.[2] The two, while remaining friends, eventually expressed reservations about each other's plays once Gorky's works began to be staged. Gorky was not very very enthusiastic about *The Three Sisters,* which premiered only in 1901, finding its mood, ideas, and characters all too familiar from Chekhov's previous dramatic efforts.[3] For his part, Chekhov discovered structural defects in each of Gorky's first two plays. Despite the two men's continuing critiques of each other's works in letters and their substantially divergent paths as dramatists, Gorky's early plays reveal an enormous debt to Chekhov.[4]

Nowhere is the extent of that debt more evident than in Gorky's first play, *The Petty Bourgeois* (*Meshchane,* 1901; also translated as *The Philistines* and *Smug Citizens*). Chekhov's basic four-act structure appears both here and in the great majority of Gorky's other full-length plays. As in Chekhov, *The Petty Bourgeois* is set in the provinces; similarly, its action centers on a single house and on a family in turmoil. Vasily Bessemenov, the well-off head of the house-painters' guild in his town, has his two grown-up children at home: Pyotr, a student expelled from the university, and Tatyana, a schoolteacher. Both are unhappy and unsettled, caught as they are between the expectations of their father and a vague desire for some better life. The tragic flaw in the Bessemenov children, as in so many of Chekhov's characters, is their inability to take themselves in hand. Like Chekhov, Gorky emphasizes situation over plot: the action moves forward not through the development of a complex intrigue but through the shifting relationships among characters experiencing a crisis in their lives. Despite Gorky's negative view of it, the Chekhov play to which *The Petty Bourgeois* seems to owe most is *The Three Sisters*. Gorky's Tatyana, who teaches school and would like to marry but seems fated to remain single, resembles Chekhov's Olga. Tatyana's unsuccessful effort to poison herself after Nil, Bessemenov's foster son, has rejected her for Polya, recalls a similar incident with Vershinin's wife in *The Three Sisters*. Polya's father, Perchikhin, quotes odd items from the newspaper, much as Chekhov's Chebutykin (7:21).

This list could easily be expanded, but to dwell too long on the similarities would create a mistaken impression. Even before the end of the first act the play displays a new and non-Chekhovian element. At first Pyotr's conflict with his father predominates, and it appears that the play will center on the family theme. But the focus quickly shifts to Nil, who berates Tatyana for her idle "philosophizing" and gives her some advice: "If you're bored with life, get involved with something. People who work aren't bored. If you don't like it at home, go and live in the country and teach, or go to Moscow and study" (7:30). The reference to Moscow is again reminiscent of the Chekhov play, and, like Chekhov's three sisters, Tatyana is not about to go anywhere. But Gorky, as the very title of his play indicates, elaborates the broad social implications of his characters' behavior more directly than Chekhov.

Nil is meant to be the play's real hero. He rejects all aspects of bourgeois society; his scorn for Tatyana's philosophizing foreshadows his decision to marry the poor Polya, as well as his departure from the Bessemenov household. Pyotr is Nil's polar opposite. Although he is in love with, and loved by, Elena Krivtsova, a woman with the energy and passion Pyotr lacks, it is hard to believe that he will ever make anything of his life. Both he and Nil are "individualists," but Pyotr represents a self-centered individualism that Gorky condemns, while Nil's independence and strength are directed toward helping others.

The social and—to the extent possible under tsarist censorship—political concerns at the core of Gorky's play tend to overwhelm the subtle psychological relationships typically seen in a Chekhov play.[5] Chekhov himself criticized the work on two other grounds. First, he felt that its structure was not quite right, that the fourth act should be placed at the beginning and the third act last.[6] The third act contains Tatyana's attempt at suicide and the immediate reactions to it, while the fourth investigates the differences in outlook among the characters and ends with an attack on the values by which the Bessemenov family has lived. Chekhov did not provide a detailed critique of the order of the acts, but it is clear that ending the play with the third act would have left the dramatic situation unresolved, as was Chekhov's wont, and would have shifted emphasis to the characters' personalities. Placing the explosive conflicts of act 4 at the beginning would have freed the rest of the drama to concentrate more on the relationships among the people, less on the social themes. Second, as one of the first to appreciate the importance of Nil, Chekhov felt that his part should have been enlarged, that of Teterev, a hanger-on at the Bessemenov household, reduced.[7] He realized that Nil was asked to carry too much of the play's message without being allowed to emerge dramatically as the chief figure.

Here in essence is the weakness of *The Petty Bourgeois*. Leonid Andreev, in a generally positive review written at about the time of its opening, noted that the play contains many events, but no "dramatic action."[8] The absence of intrigue works well for Chekhov, but Gorky's attempt to deal with both the psychological complexities of his characters and a range of social issues makes the play too dense. Andreev also remarked that all the characters are primary; there are virtually no secondary roles. Several sets of intricate relationships, based both on personality and on social concerns, swirl through the play, which lacks a center. Chekhov suggested that Nil logically should be the central character but that he had too little to say and do. Still, despite its defects, *The Petty Bourgeois* was a promising beginning in a demanding genre.

The Lower Depths

Gorky's next drama, *The Lower Depths* (*Na dne*, 1902; literally, "On the Bottom"), is universally considered his greatest play. It is the single work by which he is best known outside the Soviet Union, even though several of his other plays have been performed in the English-speaking world in recent years. Both in its setting and in its characters *The Lower Depths* is far removed from *The Petty Bourgeois*—and from Gorky's subsequent plays as well. The heroes are Gorky's "ex-people," those "Creatures That Once Were Men" of whom he wrote in his stories of the 1890s.

The setting is a lower-class lodging, a flophouse that serves as a refuge for those society has cast aside, as well as for those who have consciously rejected it. Most of the action occurs in a dirty basement illuminated by a single window. Act 3 takes place just outside the house, in a yard surrounded by walls. Thus characters live in darkness, cut off from the natural world—hence an early title for the play, *Without Sunlight (Bez solntsa)*.

The bleakness of the setting is a metaphor for the spiritual life of those who live "on the bottom." Some revel in their situation and care little for their fellows. Such is Bubnov, once a furrier. When Anna, the wife of the blacksmith Kleshch, dies, he remarks "Well, she's stopped her coughing . . . we have to tell Kleshch; it's his business" (7:147). At the same time Bubnov claims to revere "truth.": "As for me, I don't know how to lie. Why should I lie? My feeling is you should lay out the whole truth. What is there to be ashamed of?" (7:155). The Baron is much like Bubnov. He too has fallen far in life, and he expresses a similar love for truth. He joins Bubnov in mocking those, such as Natasha and the prostitute Nastya, who want to believe in a better life for themselves. At the end, though, Nastya turns the tables on him. The Baron is proud of his pedigree; in act 4, as he muses about his noble family and its possessions, Nastya declares that it is all lies, that he never had anything. The Baron, so willing to attack the dreams of others, quickly comes apart when his own vision of something better—in this case one presumably based on actual memories—is attacked.

The locksmith Kleshch stands apart from these two figures. They have reached bottom by the time the play opens, while he drifts down to their level as it unfolds.[9] His failures do not result from maliciousness or laziness—as with Bubnov and the Baron—but from an inability to cope with life's setbacks. After Bubnov's speech about truth, Kleshch exclaims: "What's truth? Where is it? [tearing at the rags he is wearing] . . . Here's what truth is! I've got no work, no strength! That's truth! I don't have a roof over my head! All that's left is to croak. . . .there's truth for you!" (7:155).

Kleshch is no hero. He has brutally beaten his wife throughout their marriage, and as she lies dying he does nothing to help her. At the end of the play he joins the other castoffs in their carousing. He is the play's object lesson. Helen Muchnic's judgment on the play's characters—what troubles them, she says, "is a sense not of guilt, but of inadequacy"[10] applies most aptly to him.

All three characters, while important within individual scenes, have less to do with the play's action that those who dream, however hopelessly, of a better life. The main intrigue involves a thief, Vaska Pepel, who courts both Vasilisa, the wife of the lodging house's owner Kostylev, and Vasilisa's sister Natasha. Pepel has been a thief from his earliest years; in the course of the play he thinks of giving up stealing, going off with Natasha to Siberia, and starting a new life. As usual, reality intrudes. After Vasilisa overhears his plans, she and her husband beat and scald Natasha. Pepel, who intervenes to defend Natasha along with the other lodgers, strikes Kostylev and kills him. Then Natasha, whose loyalty to Pepel is at best uncertain, accuses him of plotting with Vasilisa and both Vasilisa and Pepel end up in jail. At the edge of this drama and of the other action in the play stands Nastya, a streetwalker who envisions herself as a heroine of the romantic novels she reads constantly. Unable to escape from her own situation, she offers support to others. Another dreamer is a drunkard known only by the name of his former profession—the Actor. He resembles the Baron and Bubnov in his fall from previous heights, but unlike them he has not accepted failure. He and Nastya bear the brunt of their fellow lodgers' taunts; when the Actor realizes he cannot fulfill the hopes that have been rekindled in him, he hangs himself.

While Pepel, Nastya, and the Actor are at the center of the play's action, its thematic concerns are expressed more directly through two other characters—Satin, a card sharp who once killed a man and then spent some time in prison; and Luka, a wanderer who comes to the lodging house for only a short time. Luka dominates the first three acts, and Satin is the chief figure of the fourth. From the start Luka offers encouragement to others. He tells Anna that she should not fear death, for it will bring her peace at last. He persuades the Actor that there is a place where people like him can be cured of drunkenness. He advises Pepel to run off to Siberia. Many years later Gorky claimed that all Luka could offer to others was the "consoling lie." According to Gorky, Luka belonged to the most harmful category of consolers: those who are knowlegeable and eloquent but whose main concern is their own comfort. Gorky felt that his play was unsuccessful to the extent that he failed to make his opinion of Luka clear.[11]

Gorky's unease was justified. Even though Luka's ideas are attacked by other characters, he does well within the play. Perhaps Luka's vague recollection of a rehabilitation center for alcoholics engenders a fatal hope in the Actor, but otherwise he is helpful. His comforting words to Anna are not a lie but the truth: death will indeed bring her peace. And by his advice to Pepel he offers encouragement to perhaps the only inhabitant of the basement with both the will and strength to renew his life. Luka does not accept the notion that people must always have the truth. He tells of a man who believed that a righteous land existed somewhere. When it was finally proved to him that no such land existed, the man hanged himself. This story both anticipates the Actor's death at the end of the play and recalls Gorky's parable "About the Siskin Who Lied and the Woodpecker Who Loved the Truth."[12] A lie may sometimes inspire people. The truths of Bubnov and the Baron only hold people down, and may even be destructive.

Satin, to an extent Gorky's voice in the play, believes in the truth, but his truth is not Bubnov's. In the final act, after a melee during which Pepel is arrested and Luka disappears, Satin expresses his views: "Lies are the religion of slaves and bosses; truth is the God of a free man!" (7:173). A short while later he utters one of Gorky's most frequently quoted passages: "Only man exists; everything else is the creation of his hands and his brain! M-a-n! The word is magnificent; it has a proud ring to it! A man has to be respected! Not pitied . . . don't degrade him with pity. . . .You've got to respect him!" (7:177). Satin's monologues might seem to refute Luka's views, but Satin's statements are not all one-sided. His comments on Luka in fact contain as much praise as reproof. Satin points out that Luka too understood the importance of "Man," and quotes extensively from Luka's remarks to the effect that all people ultimately live for something better. Satin's imitation of Luka rivets the attention of his listeners: Nastya, Kleshch, the Baron, and the Actor all pay heed. Satin is not, as has sometimes been claimed, the opposite of Luka. That distinction belongs to Bubnov and perhaps the Baron. Like Luka, Satin wants to help people, but he offers a view of life without illusions. Nastya's novels, Pepel's plans to

leave for Siberia, the Actor's dream of a cure for his drunkenness—
Satin is skeptical about all these. He sees no easy way out, and
believes that people will be stronger for recognizing this fact.
The play's strength, as in the best of Gorky's fiction generally,
lies in its characters. Luka, Satin, the Actor, the Baron, Nastya—
all are original creations who permit experienced actors to test their
skills. Luka's role is particularly crucial; the degree to which he is
made sympathetic has a telling effect on the message conveyed in
the first three acts.[13] If the play has a flaw, it is in its structure.
Again, Chekhov was the first to elucidate this problem, in comments
he made after reading a copy of the play Gorky had sent him just
after finishing it. Chekhov basically liked the play, especially the
second act, which concludes with Anna's death. But he noted: "You
have excluded the most interesting characters (except for the Actor)
from the fourth act, and now mind lest nothing comes of it. That
act could seem boring and unnecessary, especially if with the departure of the stronger and more interesting actors only the so-so
ones remain."[14] And indeed Luka, Vaska Pepel, Vasilisa, and Natasha, the play's most important figures until then, are all missing
from the fourth act. Chekhov's criticism has received much attention. Perhaps the best effort to come to terms with it has been made
by L. M. Farber, who sees *The Lower Depths* as three plays in one.
At the core is a four-act play about the lower depths themselves,
and about the vagabonds, thieves, and other desperate people who
inhabit them. Acts 1 through 3 also contain a philosophical drama
dealing with questions of good and evil, of truth versus falsehood.
Luka plays the key role in this second play. Finally, the fourth act
is a one-act political play, a kind of authorial monologue presented
through Satin. Indirectly accepting Chekhov's critique, Farber notes
that the theatrical links among the three "plays" are weak.[15]
     Here, then, is another example of that "disunity" found in many
of Gorky's stories and novels. He strives more for density than for
consistency; in attempting to incorporate all his ideas he loses a
single focus. Hence there is a reason for the play's somewhat clouded
message and the unintentionally positive portrayal of Luka. The
philosophical concerns of the first three acts create a sympathy for
Luka that cannot be easily eliminated. Satin's alternative program
is presented only after Luka's, and since Satin interacts much less
than Luka with the other characters, his words leave a less vivid
impression than Luka's deeds. Despite its untidiness, though, the

play succeeds in the final analysis. What Farber describes as the four-act play—the psychological drama of life on the bottom—gives resonance to the ideological positions of Luka and Satin. The grimness of the setting, the uniqueness of the characters, and the constant interplay between hope and despair make *The Lower Depths* a powerful work and a remarkable achievement for a fledgling playwright.

Plays about the Intelligentsia

After *The Lower Depths* Gorky abandoned the vagabond theme, and never returned to the milieu that gave him his greatest dramatic success in his subsequent writings for the stage. His next three plays all depict the intelligentsia, and thus have frequently been discussed as a group.[16] They represent a reversion to a more Chekhovian manner, albeit as always with Gorky political and social concerns are much closer to the surface than they are in Chekhov. Like his first two plays, these contain complicated relationships, and it takes time to sort out the various characters. In *The Lower Depths,* though, the characters themselves were sufficiently interesting to carry much of the work. Here Gorky offers less variety in his characters and greater complexity of plot. But, because Gorky is less adept at creating intrigue, the three works emerge as inferior to *The Lower Depths.* Even so, individual characters and scenes in these works play quite well on the stage.

Of the three, English-speaking audiences today are likely to be familiar only with *Summerfolk* (*Dachniki,* 1904). Its characters fall roughly into three groups. Some, like the lawyer Basov and his assistant Zamyslov, seem totally at home in their corrupt society. Others—especially the intellectuals or those who aspire to intellectual pursuits—sense that something is wrong, but they are inept in their every undertaking and cut off from real life. This group includes Shalimov (a well-known writer), Ryumin, and Basov's sister Kaleria. Then there are those who understand the problems with their lives. Some—the doctor Dudakov; his wife, Olga; and Yulia, wife of the engineer Suslov—are nonetheless too weak or indecisive to act, but others—Basov's wife, Varvara; her brother Vlas; and Maria Lvovna, a doctor—reject the "summerfolk" environment and set out for a new life.

As is typical of Gorky's full-length plays, *Summerfolk* contains

four acts, and it was the first of many that Gorky subtitled "Scenes."
It is a series of loosely connected moments that create an effect more
by accumulation than by plot development. While many small
intrigues occur among the characters, the play focuses primarily on
a growing self-awareness among some characters and a growing sense
of unease among others. The main impetus for change comes from
Vlas and Maria Lvovna, who from the beginning express the greatest
distaste for the society surrounding them and who soon become an
unlikely romantic pair (she is thirty-seven; he is twenty-five). Both
separately and together they attack the failings they see in others—
Vlas somewhat sarcastically, Maria out of high-minded idealism.
Their example rouses others to action. Suslov's uncle Dvoetochie
has sold a factory and does not know what to do with himself or
his money. Under Maria Lvovna's influence he vows to put his
resources to work building schools.[17] Varvara, who has already grown
apart from Basov, seeks personal happiness outside marriage. Her
choice falls on Ryumin, a once lively individual now fearful of all
life brings. Simultaneously she looks to the writer Shalimov, whom
she once saw some eight years before, when he had a bold expression
and unruly, thick, dark hair. Unfortunately, when Shalimov appears
at the end of act 1 he is bald. His loss of hair is comically symbolic
of more serious losses: he feels that he no longer understands his
readers, that he is not in tune with the younger generation. Disappointed in both men, Varvara decides to leave.

Chekhov hovers over this play too, though this time the work
most recalled is not *The Three Sisters* but *The Seagull:* a group of
actors prepares to put on an entertainment that echoes the staging
of the play in the first act of *The Seagull;* both a writer and a would-
be author have significant parts in both works (Gorky's Shalimov
and Kaleria, Chekhov's Trigorin and Treplyov); Ryumin tries to
kill himself but inflicts only a minor wound in a way that recalls
Treplyov's first suicide attempt, and so forth.[18] Yet a comparison
of the two works immediately reveals Chekhov's relative economy.
The troupe in *Summerfolk* never plays so integral a part in the story
as the staging of Treplyov's play does in *The Seagull;* Gorky introduces not one doctor, but two; and the complexity of the relationships in Gorky's work leaves the individual characters less sharply
defined than in Chekhov's.

The second of these plays, *Children of the Sun (Deti solntsa,* 1905),
stands somewhat apart from Gorky's other dramatic work. The very

title recalls Andreev, and indeed the play originated as a joint project between Gorky and Andreev. Their working title was *The Astronomer;* when the collaboration fell through, Andreev went on to write the play *To the Stars (K zvezdam)*. Gorky returned to his play while under arrest in the Peter and Paul Fortress for his activities during "Bloody Sunday" in 1905, and his conception of the work changed as a result. [19] He focused on a chemist, Protasov, who is totally out of touch with the ordinary life that surrounds him, and on the anger of the masses that, during a cholera epidemic, is directed at all those perceived as having any connection with medicine. In its combination of the comic and the eerie, of both a dark and an optimistic vision, and in its treatment of madness and suicide, it stands as a forerunner of Gorky's plays of the 1910s.

The final play of this small cycle, *The Barbarians (Varvary,* 1905), reverts to the manner of *Summerfolk,* with its large cast of characters and numerous multisided relationships. Its unhappy pairings, in which love is rarely reciprocated, again give the play a Chekhovian mood. The action takes place in the provincial town of Verkhopole, which, there is reason to believe, is modeled on Arzamas. [20] The historical reference of the title receives a complex resonance in the play: the true barbarians are not outsiders but the local inhabitants, such as the mayor Redozubov and the lumber merchant Pritykin, whose crudeness and greed are characteristic of the provincial town. But Redozubov views the engineers who arrive from outside to help build a railroad as invaders who threaten his once unchallenged power: "These free thinkers are . . . barbarians. They're transgressors! They're overrunning everything and laying it to waste" (7:444). Redozubov's judgment contains more truth than he realizes. The engineers, Cherkun and Tsyganov, do not just lay waste to Redozubov's empire; they also have a destructive impact on the lives of many in the town. Both the insiders and the outsiders could be labeled barbarians.

In this cycle Gorky's depictions of the intelligentsia became progressively darker. In *Summerfolk* several individuals break wth the status quo and attempt to achieve some good in the world. *Children of the Sun* contains less evil but also less good; the more educated characters are not so much bad as simply ineffectual. But in *The Barbarians* all the major characters are despotic, corrupt, or weak. The Marxist critic Anatoly Lunacharsky, anxious to find some positive message in this publicistic play, noted that Stepan, a student, and Katya, Redozubov's daughter, stand apart from the rest and offer hope of a new beginning; but he had to admit that both are weakly developed.[21] In all there is little to choose between the better-educated, presumably more enlightened outsiders and those raised in the darkness of the provinces.

Transitional Works

Gorky's next play, *Enemies* (*Vragi,* 1906), written during his sojourn in the United States, marks the beginning of a period during which Gorky outgrew his reliance on Chekhovian characters and situations. He turns from the world of the dachas and the rural gentry to the newly emergent industrial society, as here, or else to the merchant class that he also depicted in his novels.

Enemies, like *Mother,* which Gorky also wrote in the United States, deals directly with revolutionary events. If *Mother* may be called the first socialist realist novel, then *Enemies* should be termed the first socialist realist play. It quickly drew the attention of such Marxist critics as Georgy Plekhanov, who praised the work for its ideological and literary merits and noted Gorky's creation of heroes out of ordinary workers.[22] The play itself, though, concentrates more on the factory owners than on the workers. Mikhail Skrobotov and his partner, Zakhar Bardin, run a large factory where worker unrest has emerged. Zakhar is Gorky's version of the typical "liberal": he prefers to avoid harsh confrontations and is willing to grant at least some of the workers' demands, but he lacks the decisiveness to make major changes. Mikhail is far more ruthless; he responds to the workers' demands by declaring a lockout and then is killed by one of his employees. Zakhar would like the workers to hand over the guilty person themselves in order to avoid further trouble, but before his death Mikhail had summoned troops. During the subsequent investigation a younger worker confesses in an effort to shield the actual murderer, who then steps forward to accept the blame.

The men in the factory are all hardworking, self-sacrificing, and honest to a fault—less fanatic, but generally much like Pavel Vlasov in *Mother.* Members of the upper classes are characterized primarily by their attitude toward the workers, which in most cases is predictable. Mikhail's widow, Cleopatra, and his brother remain hostile and uncompromising. Zakhar and his wife, Polina, do not change either. They are milder than the Skrobotovs, but they do not resist the harsh measures taken by the troops. Their attitude toward the workers consists of condescension tinged with fear. Nadya, Polina's niece, sympathizes with the workers—in some ways she is reminiscent of Katya in *The Barbarians*. But the "most dramatically viable characters," as John Simon termed them, are Zakhar's brother Yakov and Yakov's wife, Tatyana.[23] For these are the two figures most nearly in the middle. Tatyana, an actress, strongly sympathizes with the workers. She flirts with Mikhail's brother, trying unsuccessfully to persuade him to release one of the arrested workers. At the end she seems about to join with Nadya, although until then she has lacked any firm commitment in her life. Her husband, though, cannot move off dead center. He professes membership in the class that comprises the "loafers, tramps, monks, beggars, and other spongers in this world" (7:524). When he departs from Tatyana he goes—although she does not realize it at the time—to shoot himself.

The Last Ones (Poslednie, 1908) shares a political theme with *Enemies.* As a result its publication within Russia was also forbidden by the censors, though in fact both plays were occasionally performed by individual theaters in prerevolutionary Russia. The two differ in their postrevolutionary fate, with *Enemies* being much the better known of the two. Yet *The Last Ones* is not without interest. The mother of a young revolutionary falsely acused of shooting at a police official visits the man to seek mercy for her son. Her visit brings out a conflict within the official's family, which lies at the core of the play. The work is actually more of a domestic than a political drama: all four acts take place in the official's house, and nearly all the characters are related to him or his wife.

Gorky's accomplishments in the play are twofold. First, he has written a political play without political characters. The accused revolutionary never appears on stage. Thus the cause he represents primarily serves as a kind of litmus test to define individuals through their reaction to it. Second, Gorky has simplified and sharpened the intrigues. Instead of the complex interweavings of his earlier plays, a single main conflict, that between two brothers, predominates. If *Enemies* marks the end of Gorky's first period of playwriting, then *The Last Ones* opens the second.[24]

The Eccentrics (Chudaki, 1910; variously translated as *Queer People* and *Country Folk*) is also a transitional play. In some ways it harks back to Gorky's earlier work. Like *Summerfolk* it is set in a dacha;

the events center on a love triangle (with several subsidiary triangles as well); and there is little real action.[25] Yet the play marks an important step forward in Gorky's dramatic writing, the last stage before his "morality plays" of the 1910s. Despite the many external similarities to *Summerfolk,* the differences are more important. Nearly all Gorky's early plays are to a large extent sociological tracts—they concentrate on the failings of educated, well-to-do Russians, and they value characters in accordance with the extent to which they rebel against their own world. The writer Shalimov *(Summerfolk),* who accepts society's mores and totally fails to understand the new types of people he observes, is a wholly negative figure. In *The Eccentrics,* which contains far fewer characters and relegates social issues to the background, the writer Mastakov, who strives to convey a positive vision, is a much more attractive, if hardly ideal, person. Psychological and philosophical issues are in the foreground.

On the surface not much happens in the play. Mastakov, an established writer, and his wife Elena are at a dacha, where Mastakov begins to flirt with Olga, a woman with a considerable past. Elena meanwhile has attracted the attention of Nikolai Potekhin, a doctor and a longtime friend of Mastakov's. But where Mastakov is sincere, ardent, and almost naive in his enthusiasms, Potekhin is cynical, vain, and burned out. At a neighboring house a young woman, Zina, is caring for her fiancé, Vasya, who has long been ill. In the fourth and final act, after Vasya dies, Mastakov inadvertently flirts with Zina: he half realizes that the occasion is ridiculously inappropriate, but he cannot stop himself until Zina leaves. Olga realizes when Elena points it out to her that she could never put up with Mastakov's vagaries. At the end Elena and Mastakov are once more together, while Potekhin, defeated in his efforts to drive a wedge between husband and wife, leaves for parts unknown.

Of great importance as psychological studies in the play are the few secondary characters. For instance, others in the play initially admire Vasya for his courage in facing imminent death, but in fact he turns out to be querulous and bitter. The process of dying can bring out the worst rather than the best in people. Elena, who at first seems helpless before Olga's efforts to lure her husband away, possesses more strength than others realize. She understands Mastakov better than he understands himself, and in their two confrontations toward the end of the play she routs Olga.

The work's most complex figure, though, is Mastakov. On the

one hand he tries to offer his readers "goodness and beauty" (significantly, neither Potekhin nor Vasya likes the manuscript he reads to them). In his own life, though he often acts irresponsibly. As a writer, Mastakov recalls the Siskin from Gorky's parable: he wants to inspire people to live a better life. But then why does he so nearly destroy his own marriage? He offers an explanation toward the very end: "I often play the role of the holy fool who does not understand his own deeds—that helps me a lot in distancing myself from the banal and the petty" (13:149). His explanation does not totally excuse his behavior, but, as he says later on in his monologue, his very childlike qualities enable him to see in life the things that others miss. There may, indeed, be no more likely explanation for the ability of certain writers to create works of great aesthetic value while leading less than exemplary lives. For all his contradictions and at times absurd egotism, Mastakov remains one of Gorky's more profound dramatic creations.[26]

The Morality Plays

During the 1910s Gorky continued and refined the tendencies that emerged in *Children of the Sun* and developed in the plays he wrote over the next several years. He concentrates on a few characters and only one or two plot-lines instead of the multisided relationships of his early plays. The evolution from Shalimov to Mastakov represents another change. Whereas previously the central characters rarely appear in a positive light, in the later works his heroes are more sympathetic. After *The Eccentrics* his heroes, interestingly, often belong to the merchant class. As in *The Eccentrics,* though, social and political issues are largely secondary: rather, Gorky brings specific moral issues to the fore.

The Zykovs (*Zykovy,* 1912–13) was written at a time when Gorky was harshly critical of the Moscow Art Theater for its staging of works based on Dostoevsky's *Brothers Karamazov* and *The Possessed.* He apparently had previously indicated to Vladimir Nemirovich-Danchenko, the theater's codirector, that he would offer it his latest play. Angered, however, by the theater's adaptations of Dostoevsky's novels, Gorky imposed such restrictions on the staging of his work that Nemirovich-Danchenko was bound to refuse *The Zykovs.*[27] Some critics have thus seen the play as a veiled attack on Dostoevsky, or at least on two ideas important in his work: the spiritual goodness associated with meekness, and the tendency for certain people to rebel, often seemingly without reason, against society's norms.[28] It is also, in fact, possible to see an attack on Tolstoyanism in *The Zykovs*.

In some ways *The Zykovs* resembles Gorky's early tale "On a Raft." Mikhail Zykov, a weak and indecisive young man, is to be married off to Pavla, a girl who has lived for some years in a convent. Mikhail's father, Antipa, intervenes to marry Pavla himself. Like Pritykin in *The Barbarians*, Antipa is a lumber merchant, but he is less crude than either Pritykin or Silan Petrov in "On a Raft." Toward the end of the play he points out that he has made mistakes in his life, but at least he loves work and has accomplished something, unlike his son. His confession recalls that of Mastakov at the end of *The Eccentrics:* his deeds explain, and to some extent are explained by, his failings in his family duties. In the course of the play Antipa's sister Sofia, a widow, rejects two suitors and becomes the de facto head of the family business, while Antipa finds himself more and more involved with the burden of his marriage to Pavla. Mikhail eventually renews his interest in Pavla, and she responds. After a confrontation between Antipa and Mikhail, the latter shoots himself. Not seriously wounded, he is reconciled to his father, who in turn draws closer to his sister. With the whole family now united, Pavla, the greatest source of friction among the blood relations, is asked to leave.

The main concerns of the play are brought out through the three central figures. Pavla, for all her Dostoevskian meekness, has a devastating effect on those around her: she drives Antipa and others to distraction by her very goodness. Sofia, toward the end of act 2, expresses another aspect of his theme: she wants to rise above people and then declare that they do not need any masters, nor should they fear anyone (13:326). She takes the Gorkian (and anti-Dostoevskian) position of advocating strength and pride in the self. Sofia is the strongest and probably the most attractive figure in the play. Having married a dying man at her brother's behest, she spends her widowhood helping with the business. Placing her brother and the welfare of the enterprise above any personal happiness, she rejects two suitors. Her dedication to work and her determination set her apart from even her brother; Gorky clearly admires her ability to accomplish much in the world[29]

Zykov is a more problematical figure. On the one hand, his

physical stamina and industry enable him to build a successful business from which many benefit. At the same time he takes what he wants from those around him and ruthlessly crushes his own son. In the end Gorky comes down on the side of strength: Antipa justifies his treatment of his son by the latter's weakness, while Sofia and Antipa together see themselves as two struggling individuals whose wealth and success prove they are correct. The play's message would be anathema to both Dostoevsky and Tolstoy: the weak and the humble are useless; humanity advances through pride and strength.

Perhaps Gorky's most unusual play is *The Counterfeit Coin (Fal'-shivaia moneta,* 1913/1926), a work closely related to his last pre-revolutionary play, *The Old Man.* The main characters in *The Counterfeit Coin* are Polina, wife of the watchmaker Yakovlev, and Stogov, a man who wronged her some years before. Stogov becomes a lodger in the house where Yakovlev has his shop and evinces an interest in counterfeiters. He renews his acquaintance with Polina until he is diverted by her stepdaughter Natasha. Polina has suffered as Yakovlev's wife. Although he did rescue her at a bad moment, he is harsh by nature—his lack of an eye is the physical analogue of his moral deficiencies. (Yakovlev is apparently based on a real-life person, a suitor of Gorky's mother, who appears fleetingly in *Childhood.*) Polina's hopes as well as her fears are awakened by Stogov's return into her life; when his infidelity as well as his continued presence remind her of all she has endured, she kills herself.

A bare outline can only hint at the play's depth. Gorky made the plot intentionally murky, a point he emphasized upon reworking the 1913 version during the mid-1920s. He kept the first two acts largely intact but significantly revised the third (like *Enemies, The Counterfeit Coin* has just three acts). He also added one new character (Luzgin), dropped another, altered several names, and reworked the play's major figures: Stogov, Polina, Natasha,[30] The key change involves the relationship of Polina and Stogov toward the end of the play. In the 1913 version the character who evolved into Stogov was himself a counterfeiter. Greatly affected by Polina's inner goodness, as the play ends he is about to embark with her upon a new and no doubt happy life. In the final version Polina's fate has clearly changed, as has Stogov's character. The play's German translator, unsure of Gorky's intentions in several areas, once asked him for clarification. In his reply Gorky began by stating outright that

Stogov was a detective and had appeared in the town in order to catch counterfeiters.[31] In the play itself, though, Stogov's role is not so clear. At one point he tells Natasha that he is a detective, but she does not entirely believe him, nor can the viewer be completely sure of this either. And there are other mysteries too. Natasha turns out to be the daughter of Kemskoy, owner of the house, and not of Yakovlev; Polina's past appears only in fragments and is never fully elucidated; Luzgin, whose mien is abnormal from the start, talks constantly about an inheritance, but his mental illness becomes obvious only at the very end.

The issues at the heart of the play are such as to suggest the influence of the greatest Italian dramatist of the time, Pirandello.[32] While Gorky's original conception may have owed something to Pirandello's stories, his reworking of the play brought it closer in spirit to Pirandello's major works of the 1920s, most notably *Six Characters in Search of an Author* (1921); we should recall that both versions were completed during periods when Gorky was living in Italy, and he no doubt was familiar with Pirandello's work. *The Counterfeit Coin* is Gorky's only play to deal at length with illusion and reality. Two outsiders enter the Kemskoy household: Stogov and then Luzgin. At first it is difficult to see any link between the mysterious but obviously informed Stogov and the crazed Luzgin. But in act 3 the connection becomes clear. Luzgin, who has ostensibly come to have a watch repaired, is no longer sure of his own identity, or anyone else's. In the final scene he points to a mirror and blames the person in it for all the ills that have befallen him. Stogov too is trying to determine identities—to find out who the counterfeiters are, to learn the true nature of the people in the house. But he is no more successful than Luzgin. In order to distinguish a counterfeit coin from a real one, he must mark it with a needle. As he says to Natasha, "With people it's the same; you can distinguish a real person from the false ones only if you've placed your mark on him. But that spoils him." (13:273). Discovering what is real in the world presents a challenge beyond the powers of those in this play.

The Old Man (Starik) has been dated 1915 on the basis of a 1921 listing by Gorky, but there is some reason to believe that he wrote most of it as late as 1917.[33] In any case, it was the last play Gorky wrote until the final years of his career. Its hero is the merchant Mastakov, a nicer version of Antipa Zykov. He had once been unjustly accused of murder and sentenced to hard labor, from which he had escaped to start life anew in a provincial town. Pitirim, a fellow prisoner who served out his term and now wanders about as a tramp, returns to seek retribution from Mastakov. By retribution, though, Pitirim means neither punishment nor money; rather he wants to see Mastakov suffer in a way that will lower him to Pitirim's level. Caught in a hopeless trap, Mastakov finds only one way out—suicide.

Gorky's previous two plays had also presented sufferers. Polina *(The Counterfeit Coin)* is simply a victim who does not seem to deserve her fate. And in Pavla *(The Zykovs)* Gorky depicted a woman who used meekness as a weapon against others. Pitirim, though, is hardly a meek sufferer. His life has no doubt been difficult, but he revels in his own abasement. His conflict with Mastakov has been seen as a direct response to Dostoevsky's Dmitry Karamazov on Gorky's part.[34] Dmitry is convicted of a crime he did not commit, and *The Brothers Karamazov* implies that suffering can in some cases purify the individual. Dostoevsky, of course, seeks a higher goal; he did not believe in suffering merely for its own sake. Gorky, though, denies outright that suffering may have any value. More important he also—here, as in his other plays of the 1910s—rejects the right of one individual to pass judgment on another. Pavla's judgments only create dissension; Stogov finally realizes that he is an inadequate judge; while Pitirim's attempts to assume the role of judge only destroy a good person and lead to his own defeat.

Gorky worked steadily and intensely as a playwright over the first two decades of his literary career. Along with all his other writing, he readied a dozen full-length plays for publication. At least one other long play, *Yakov Bogomolov*, remained unpublished during Gorky's lifetime. What is most notable about his dramatic writing, however, is not so much the sheer volume of his output as his steady evolution. The plays of his early period—*Summerfolk, Enemies,* and especially *The Lower Depths*—tend to be his best known in the English-speaking world, and yet his later works are certainly of interest as well. They reveal a constant search for new themes; they explore further aspects of human nature; and display a level of accomplishment scarcely inferior to that found in his earlier writing.

Chapter Five
Re-creating the Past: Autobiography and Memoirs
The Autobiographical Trilogy

From the start Gorky's writing contained a strong autobiographical element. His early tales drew upon observations during years of wandering throughout Russia, and *The Lower Depths* is a virtual catalogue of the types he came across while living among the dregs of Russian society. Similarly, his first two novels, *Foma Gordeev* and *The Three of Them,* depict the environment of his youth. Then for several years, beginning shortly before 1905, Gorky's work relied less on his own experiences. During this period he wrote the cycle of plays depicting middle-class intellectuals, and also composed his political novels (*Mother, The Life of a Useless Man*), which describe events he knew largely at second hand. He began to revert to his earlier approach with *A Confession*; while hardly autobiographical, it does provide an indirect account of Gorky's inner turmoil at the time of writing. Then in the Okurov cycle, in particular *The Life of Matvei Kozhemiakin,* Gorky returned to the region and the people he knew well.

His work on that novel in the early 1910s marked the beginning of an intensive effort to explore the significant events of his life, one that continued well into the 1920s. The most famous product of this effort is the three-part "autobiographical trilogy" (*Childhood, In the World, My Universities*), which many regard as his crowning achievement. In these years he also published two major collections of largely autobiographical sketches and stories, *Through Russia* and *Fragments from a Diary*. While their literary value is uneven, both include very fine individual pieces. During the late 1910s and early 1920s Gorky also produced literary portraits of notable people he had met, in some cases revising and expanding memoirs begun years before. Several of these memoirs—particularly those on Tolstoy, Chekhov, and Andreev—are on a par with the best of his writings.[1]

Gorky's particular combination of talents was especially suited to autobiography. His fictional works contain very effective passages devoted to describing characters—Chelkash and Konovalov, Foma Gordeev and Matvei Kozhemiakin, Luka and Antipa Zykov, and others. He is also skilled at creating gripping scenes, such as the climax of "Twenty-Six Men and a Girl," the wedding of Savely Kozhemiakin and Palaga, or the clash between Mastakov and Pitirim in *The Old Man*. At the same time Gorky's tales tend to exceed the confines of a single story line and become diffuse. He also moralizes to an excessive degree.

In his autobiographical writing, however, Gorky retains his strengths and overcomes his weaknesses. Since memoirs and reminiscences usually lack plot of the conventional sort, description plays a more central role in them. Time and again Gorky brings to vivid life those he once knew and recreates memorable incidents of his youth. The discursive narration that disturbs some readers of Gorky's fiction is less bothersome in memoirs, which presumably follow the course of actual experience. Furthermore, when dealing with his own observations Gorky is more prepared to let his impressions speak for themselves and avoid moralizing.

Gorky's earliest attempt to write about himself directly dates from 1893, when he began and then abandoned "An Account of the Facts and Thoughts Whose Interaction Dried Up the Best Parts of My Heart" ("Izlozhenie faktov i dum, ot vzaimodeistviia kotorykh vysokhli luchshie kuski moego serdtsa," 1:451–67).[2] This piece describes several events later presented in *Childhood*, but when he began to write that work some twenty years later he could not find the notebook containing his "Account," and so began afresh.[3] On Capri, however, Gorky did not plunge immediately into what was to become his autobiographical trilogy, but began with various shorter pieces, several of which he eventually incorporated into *Through Russia*. It was as though Gorky were constrained to begin gradually, to explore individual corners of his past before presenting his youthful experiences in their entirety.

Especially important in this regard are two items of 1912, the year before he began the serial publication of *Childhood*. Both deal with the Kazan period. In "An Incident from the Life of Makar" ("Sluchai iz zhizni Makara") Gorky employs a third-person narration to describe his attempt at suicide in December of 1887. He avoids the first person partly, of course, to establish a distance enabling him to analyze this event with a sense of perspective. He even manages a touch of irony in his description of Makar's efforts to compose a suitable suicide note; one draft after another proves unsatisfactory, and then Makar is interrupted by a young woman who regards his declaration of suicidal intent as simply boring. Another circumstance may also have motivated Gorky to choose a third-person narrative. In his trilogy the introspective passages tend to be short and fairly widely distributed; Gorky deals with the "self," but his personality and thoughts emerge mostly through his reactions to others. Gorky somehow avoided the self-examination necessary to explain his suicide attempt when writing in the first person. By transposing the event to a "third person," Gorky could accept the painful incident, and then deal with it directly, though only fleetingly, in the third part of his trilogy.

The other work immediately preceding *Childhood* is "The Boss" ("Khoziain"). Here Gorky writes not just about the city, but also about the profession (baking) that inspired some of his finest fiction. In its manner and content "The Boss" clearly foreshadows the trilogy. It is certainly autobiographical. Vasily Semenov, the "boss" of the title, who appears under his own name, owned a bakery in which Gorky worked during the mid-1880s. A newspaper report has been found that corroborates Gorky's account at the story's end of Vasily Semenov's bankruptcy and flight from his creditors.[4] In addition, at least a few of the other characters had definite real-life prototypes.[5]

The work's attraction lies in Gorky's skill at presenting what appear to be, and very possibly were, real incidents in all their natural disjointedness and molding them into a narrative that subtly yet surely creates a comprehensive picture of the environment in which he lived at the time. The boss himself—ugly and rotund, a libertine with women and harsh with his employees—would seem to be fully characterized by his almost grotesque appearance when the narrator first sees him. But, Semenov's depiction is not totally one-sided. In his conversations with the narrator and in his semi-effectual attempts to control others he emerges as a relatively complex, if hardly admirable, figure. The story's major event—the poisoning of some pigs that Semenov keeps, followed by a fight among the workers in the bakery with a serious injury to the youngest of them, an eleven-year-old-boy—is quite dramatic, but it also captures the rhythm of these people's lives. The explosion is followed by an oppressive calm: the injured boy goes to a hospital but survives, contrary to all expectations, and life resumes its normal course until the next major yet temporary disruption. In many ways, "The Boss" is a polished work and a clear experiment in the manner that Gorky employed so effectively in his trilogy. What is lacking is a more detailed presentation of the self. The narrator is an active observer, but still primarily a lens to view the action rather than the focus of the work.

At the beginning of chapter 2 of *Childhood* Gorky claims, "I am not telling about myself, but about that close, stifling circle of horrible impressions in which the ordinary Russian lived and continues to live" (15:20). This point is echoed by many of those who have written about the autobiography.[6] Without a doubt much of what Gorky writes has documentary value for an understanding of life in provincial Russia during the latter part of the nineteenth century. Nevertheless, throughout his autobiography Gorky manipulates facts, transposes events, and even invents characters. Had his main intention been simply to provide a factual account of his life, he would not have taken such liberties. Gorky subordinates precise chronology and absolute factual veracity to a different goal: an analysis of his own growth, first from an unformed child into an independent but undirected youth, and then into an incipient revolutionary.

Of the autobiography's three parts the most striking is *Childhood* (*Detstvo*, 1913), probably Gorky's finest achievement. This first section is elegantly constructed: it begins with the death and funeral of Maxim Peshkov in 1871, when his son Alexei, the future Gorky, was only three, and ends with the funeral of Alexei's mother in 1879. Very likely Gorky's earliest memories were of his father's death, so the decision to start the work with it was only natural. The death of his mother, who by then was only indirectly responsible for his upbringing, seems to have had a less traumatic impact on the boy, for the adult Gorky did not originally plan to end *Childhood* at that point.[7] His later decision to do so helped shape the rest of the first part, which divides into two roughly equal halves chronicling the main stages of Gorky's boyhood. Chapters 1 through 6 depict the violence and dreariness of the environment in which Alexei is raised. He spends his early years in the home of his maternal grandparents, Vasily and Akulina Kashirin. His grandfather is already in his mid-sixties by the time Alexei and his mother return to Nizhny Novgorod from Astrakhan, where Maxim Peshkov has died of cholera contracted from his son. The owner of a large dye shop, Vasily Kashirin was a respected citizen of the town, but at about this time quarrels between him and his sons Yakov and Mikhail began to tear the family apart.[8] In the course of his childhood Alexei witnesses the gradual dissolution of both the business and the household as his grandparents sink into poverty. During the second section, chapters 8 through 13, Alexei detaches himself from the Kashirins. Chapter 7 is a watershed. Its contrast between "grandfather's God" and "grandmother's God" summarizes two ways of coping with the world in which Alexei is growing up. At the same time the descriptions in that chapter of the people whom Alexei meets on the streets of Nizhny Novgorod foreshadow the dominant concerns of the second part, and point to a third way of dealing with his surroundings.

In the first chapters of *Childhood* Alexei feels close to only three individuals: Grigory, a workman in his grandfather's enterprise who gradually loses his sight; the powerful but childlike Tsyganok ("Gypsy"); and his grandmother, Akulina Kashirina. In his earliest memories his grandmother enters his life just as his father dies, and to a degree she takes the place of both parents. His mother is rarely at home, and the boy finds himself attracted to his grandmother for her gentle kindness, which sets her apart from others he knows, her passive acceptance of her grim existence, and her skill as a teller of fairy tales. Neither Grigory nor Tsyganok fares as well as Akulina. Even though Grigory is the shop's foreman and helped found the business, Vasily lets him go once his vision fails, and Grigory ends as a blind beggar. Tsyganok, like Grigory, is too loyal: he dies while literally bearing the cross for one of Alexei's uncles (who, as an act of penance, was supposed to carry it himself to the grave of the wife he had mistreated and possibly killed). Clearly, neither Tsyganok's physical strength nor the manual skill of Grigory ensures survival in this society. Akulina endures, but she too suffers a series of defeats in chapters 4 through 6: she burns her hands fighting a fire and then watches helplessly as her daughter-in-law dies in childbirth; her husband beats her viciously; and finally her own son breaks her arm. The grandmother accepts her troubles with equanimity, but Alexei becomes increasingly uncomfortable with her passivity and soon grows away from her.

The child's relationship with his grandfather is complex and ultimately no less vital to him than that with his grandmother. On the one hand Alexei is repelled by Grandfather's cruelty: the head of the Kashirin clan is quick to administer punishment and stingy with expressions of kindness. Yet Grandfather turns out to be less wicked than the boy at first imagines. He pays a kind visit to his grandson after flogging him (chapter 2), and in chapter 5 he even tells Alexei stories of his own. Gorky claims that his grandfather "never told me any fairy tales, but only things that had actually taken place" (15:73). But Grandfather's stories are less authentic than Gorky lets on. For instance, Vasily Kashirin's story that his own father had been cut to pieces by a band of robbers (15:71) turns out to be false: his father was killed, but apparently while serving as a soldier fighting Napoleon's troops.[9] The difference between Grandfather and Grandmother is not that of realist versus romantic: each presents a vision of the world that incorporates a highly subjective perception.

The contrast between the grandparents lies rather in the content of the vision each offers, and nowhere is that distinction sharper than in the nature of the God each worships. As becomes clear in the pivotal seventh chapter, Grandmother's concept of God implies at least the possibility of greater individual freedom. He is neither all-seeing nor all-powerful, but pities people, who must endure evil and suffering. He is a God from whom one can seek comfort even while seeking to escape from or overturn the existing order of things. Grandfather's God, on the other hand, is both omnipotent and unforgiving. He demands constant attendance and obedience, allowing no room for any independence. To the extent that the Kashirins follow this God, Alexei must sever his ties with the family to have any chance at all. From the start the people to whom Alexei feels closest are not Kashirins: his grandmother is one only by marriage, while both Grigory and Tsyganok lack any Kashirin blood. Alexei himself may be a blood relation, but, in Tsyganok's words, he comes to regard himself as a Peshkov, not a Kashirin. Although he has only the vaguest memory of his father, he uses his father's name as a way of asserting his independence from the Kashirin household.

To gain independence, however, he must break with his grandmother as well as his grandfather. Grandmother serves as the fixed point in *Childhood* against which the changes in Alexei are measured: indeed at one point Gorky considered calling his book *Grandmother*.[10]

Alexei openly disagrees with her for the first time over their lodger, "Good Idea" (Khoroshee delo): she does not like him because he is different, while Gorky is attracted to him for precisely that reason. When Akulina is beaten again by her husband in chapter 10, she does not want her grandson to say anything. Alexei nevertheless takes revenge by cutting up his grandfather's favorite church calendar: by now he not only questions his grandmother's passivity but dares to act on his own. At this point he needs someone other than his grandmother as a model. Significantly, Akulina, who earlier had replaced his father in his life, now restores his father to him: almost all of chapter 11 consists of her stories about his father. In them she depicts a spirited Maxim Peshkov, who contrasts with the weak, mean-tempered Kashirins. At the end of the chapter Alexei imagines his father not in the company of his grandmother, who had felt close to Maxim, but as a person always alone, an embodiment of the independence Alexei seeks.

Alexei then tries to protect his mother from his new stepfather, that interloper taking the place of his dead father. During an argument the stepfather attacks Alexei's mother. The boy picks up a knife—the only possession of his father's that his mother still owned, Gorky tells us—and attempts to stab his stepfather with it (15:192–93). Having almost literally taken over for his father, he adopts his father's independent manner as well. In the final chapter of *Childhood* Alexei consorts with street youths, foreign to the more respectable world of the Kashirins. When the death of his mother destroys his blood tie to the Kashirin household, he abandons his childhood home to go out into the world.

Several qualities contribute to the power of the first part of Gorky's biography. One is that childhood is a special period for the autobiographer; the earliest memories are nearly always of a time of innocence, and a writer like Gorky can use the awakening from innocence to the real world to create a contrast that makes both stand out in relief.[11] Gorky's fond recollections of his grandmother, his few good moments with his grandfather, and even the occasional high spirits of his dissolute Uncle Yakov all represent a childhood happiness that reality has taken away. Second, Gorky modifies people and events to create a work of striking symmetry and with clearcut moral values. Several individuals appear at suspiciously convenient moments in the narrative. Thus in his "Account" Gorky makes no mention of Tsyganok, even when describing a flogging during which Tsyganok plays an important role in *Childhood*. Similarly, Good Idea is absent from that earlier chronicle but enters *Childhood* at a crucial point in Alexei's development. Even if prototypes of these figures—as well as of others such as Grigory and the cabdriver Petya—existed, their precise depictions and the timing of their appearances in *Childhood* must owe something to the exigencies of the narrative. Moreover, Gorky favors extreme types, whether totally positive (Good Idea, Tsyganok) or totally negative (his mother's suitors, Petya). When other sources can be checked, Gorky apparently made his characters less ambiguous by accentuating good or bad features. Twenty years earlier, in his "Account," Gorky had described his grandmother as follows: "grandmother's gaze did not bother me at all, because she loved me and also because she was often drunk. She drank a great deal and once almost died as a result. I remember them throwing water over her while she was lying in bed; her face was blue and she had vacant, terrible, lusterless eyes. I also loved her very much; she was always so kind and amusing and was so good at telling me wonderful fairy tales that frightened me" (1:464). In *Childhood* Gorky refers to his grandmother's drinking only briefly and does not mention the fact that her fairy tales frightened him. Even though he rejects her passive acceptance of all life brings, he nonetheless invests her with an aura of goodness that virtually transforms her into a fairy-tale heroine herself.

In fact, a magical fairy-tale atmosphere pervades the entire work. The most obvious folk element consists of the grandmother's tales and legends, which greatly influence her grandson and account in large measure for the adult Gorky's interest in folklore. Perhaps the polarity between good and evil in the memoir derives from his fascination with fairy tales. There are also more subtle instances of folk influence. For example, events in Alexei's own life occur with the suddenness and seeming mystery of fairy tales: "Grandfather unexpectedly sold the house to a barkeeper" (15:98); "And then, I don't remember how, I found myself in Sormovo" (15:183); "Once again I was living with Grandfather" (15:194). Toward the end this aura begins to dissipate. The disgusting tales of the cabdriver Petya cause Alexei to alter his attitude toward invented stories; his mother's decline and death mar his image of her. Yet even the undermining of the memoir's fairy-tale qualities bears witness to their pervasiveness in *Childhood*.[12]

The rest of the autobiography, while certainly among Gorky's

finer achievements, nonetheless seems a little pale by comparison
with *Childhood*. *In the World* (*V liudiakh,* 1914–16; also translated
as *My Apprenticeship*) contains many memorable portraits, but it lacks
any single individual who guides the boy's development. Gorky's
grandparents appear in this second section, but here the boy sees
them only sporadically and they gradually fade into the background.
For the most part Alexei moves from one menial job to the next.
At regular intervals he returns to work for a cousin, V. A. Sergeev,
who, however, remains less individualized than any of the main
characters in *Childhood*. Many of the other figures, who may touch
his life only briefly, ultimately blend into one another. It is characteristic that not one but several individuals should remind him
of Good Idea; and Alexei's experiences, though striking when taken
individually, after a while repeat themselves.[13] The fairy-tale atmosphere, still present at the beginning of *In the World,* gradually
yields to a clear but harsh realistic manner.

Events are often paired in such a way as to impart symmetry to
the work, but *In the World* lacks the clear structural divisions of
Childhood. Thus Alexei's work in a shoe store with his cousin Sasha
at the very beginning of *In the World* is balanced by a meeting with
Sasha's father, Yakov, at the end; Alexei is influenced by the cook
Smury when he works on one ship and by the vaguely similar
Shumov, a stoker, on another; he turns up amid a motley group of
icon painters at one point and then a short while later finds himself
in charge of an equally diverse gang of workmen at the Nizhny
Novgorod fairground. On the other hand, Alexei's development
during this period of his life is more gradual; it is difficult to trace
the changes he undergoes or even to say in what way he is different
at the end from what he was at the beginning. The young Alexei
does read a lot, and the list of books he devours throughout *In the
World* bears witness to his growing literary awareness.[14] But reading
by itself is not a sufficiently dynamic theme to sustain a work of
several hundred pages. Part 2 of the autobiography, while engaging
in its individual scenes, is relatively undramatic.

The Sergeev family, which employs Alexei at various times, is
simply dull, with a weak, uncultured husband, Vasily, and a wife
who sings the same song over and over again until Alexei is convinced
that it is the only one she knows (15:328).[15] Earlier on his world
still contained elements of mystery. While an apprentice in the shoe
store, he is approached by a rather sinister old man who wants

Alexei to steal a pair of boots; it is never clear whether the old man is serious or not. His coworker, Sasha, proudly shows him a small shrine built around the corpse of a sparrow he had suffocated. When he is back with his grandparents for a short interval, he goes for wonderful walks with his grandmother in the woods, and then becomes enchanted with the lame Lyudmila, who induces him to read a long sentimental novel with her.[16] But, his arrival in the Sergeev household effectively ends the dreamlike quality of his narrative: the very banality of their existence swallows up his previous vision.

Nevertheless, the young Alexei soon gains an appreciation of literature and becomes conscious of his place in the world. He makes up stories based on his extensive reading of nineteenth-century authors, especially Alexandre Dumas père. In retelling (and recasting) these works he absorbs lessons that, he later feels, enabled him to avoid the worst of the evils surrounding him. But an offhand remark by the stoker Shumov makes him realize that his favorite novels have nothing to say about the details of ordinary life (15:395), and this is an important lesson. Alexei later remarks on the distinction between peasants in books and peasants in real life (15:487): those in books are either entirely good or bad and in either case their personalities are fully expressed within the story, whereas in real life peasants are neither all good nor all bad, but infinitely more interesting. Thus Alexei not only reads a lot during this time, but also develops the ability to gauge the quality of a work. Yet as his self-education progresses, his situation remains unsettled. He no longer has either the gang of boys with which he roamed at the end of *Childhood* nor any older people with whom to associate. He is an orphan not just because he has no parents, but because there are no adults to guide him through life.[17]

The high point of Alexei's literary education comes between the two voyages he describes. A well-off young woman, a lodger in the house where his cousin lives, introduces him to the works of Pushkin and other major Russian writers. He calls her Queen Margot after the heroine of the Dumas novel *La Reine Margot*. But, for all her interest in educating Alexei, her personal life is a series of love intrigues, and he quickly realizes that she moves in a different world. His sense of alienation grows particularly strong during the last third of *In the World*. Alexei works for a while in a shop that produces icons, and while he meets a few people there who are worthy of admiration, he does not feel close to any of them. Later, after his cousin has put him in charge of some workers at the fairgrounds, he becomes fascinated with the personality of the carpenter Osip, but the workman remains as much a mystery to Alexei as were Smury, Shumov, and others.

Death is equally incomprehensible to him. Life, he knows, is brutal and frequently short. In *Childhood* his father and mother both died young, and his siblings did not survive past infancy. Tsyganok, Petya, and others he knows die suddenly and often prematurely. The same holds true here: a cook in the shop where he is apprenticed, his remaining infant brother, and his stepfather are among those whose deaths he witnesses. Death too serves to isolate him. Family and friends die off rapidly, leaving him more and more alone. Eventually death becomes so common as to be unworthy of comment. In *My Universities* even the news of his grandmother's death in Nizhny Novgorod while he is in Kazan comes as only a distant echo. He does not bother to mention his grandfather's death, which occurs just a few months later. Nevertheless, these deaths are a constant reminder of the harshness of his life, a harshness with which he has yet to come to terms.

My Universities (*Moi universitety,* 1923) differs as much in tone and form from *In the World* as the latter does from *Childhood.* Throughout *In the World* Alexei still seems boyish—an older child, but a child nonetheless. By the beginning of *My Universities* he is very much a young man. Even though this third section of the autobiography begins where the previous part ends, the narrator has changed considerably. Perhaps the passage of some six years between Gorky's completion of *In the World* and the start of *My Universities* is partly responsible for the discontinuity.

The title is ironic. Gorky went to Kazan in the vain hope of entering that city's prominent university, but his limited education and his need to support himself soon put an end to his dreams of a formal higher education. Thus his "universities" turned out to be the streets of Kazan and the political circles he joined there. *My Universities* has two quite distinct sections. The first, somewhat longer one, deals with Gorky's stay in Kazan (1884–88); the second describes his involvement with a circle of populist activists some thirty miles downriver from Kazan during the spring and summer of 1888. During this period Gorky's rejection of his society moved from the instinctive to the conscious level. His interest in politics sprang from a desire not merely to escape, but to change the existing order. Nevertheless, while attracted to the discussions and intrigues of illegal political movements, Gorky evidently played no leading part in any of the movements to which he belonged. Indeed, his tale is less the diary of a political novice than an evocative street guide to the Kazan of impoverished students and would-be students. The locales range from the "Marusovka," a long, decaying building that houses society's dregs, through Semenov's bakery (described in "The Boss"), to the bakery on Bolshaya Lyadskaya Street operated by Andrei Derenkov in order to provide support for both political circles and needy youth in Kazan. All though the book Gorky displays an easy familiarity with the city's geography and argot: for instance "Voskresenskaya Street students" are those from the university, while seminarians are referred to as "Arskoe Field students" (16:39).[18] Alexei comes across new people as well as new places at every turn: the Derenkov family, a traveling Tolstoyan, the student activist Gury Pletnev, and the teenage Marxist Nikolai Fedoseev, among many others. This chaos of impressions evidently overwhelmed Alexei, for he abruptly decided to leave for the quieter village of Krasnovidovo, where he assists the efforts of Mikhail Romas—whom he had met while in Kazan—to propagandize the peasants.[19] After the murder of a sympathetic peasant and a fire that destroys the shop in which Romas's operations are based, the center breaks up. Romas leaves to continue his revolutionary work elsewhere, while Gorky and another member of the group, Barinov, head for the Caspian Sea and the travels that inspired many of Gorky's stories.

Although the individual portraits and descriptions in *My Universities* are hardly inferior to those found in the first two parts of Gorky's autobiography, its narrative is skeletal. The segment of Gorky's life covered is about the same length as that dealt with in *In the World,* yet the former work is less than half the latter's length. Also, Alexei himself becomes more distant than before, as his thoughts and actions yield center stage to the descriptions of others. This latter development is common in autobiographies, where the adult figure often seems less fully realized than the child.[20] The sketchy quality of *My Universities* may stem from Gorky's having already mined this period for several outstanding works, including "Konovalov" and "Twenty-Six Men and a Girl," as well as for the autobiographical "Boss" and "An Incident from the Life of Makar."

Gorky seems unwilling to explore in greater detail incidents that he has already described. Instead of delving into the motivation or the aftermath of his attempted suicide, he merely refers his readers to the story about Makar. This reticence of Gorky's about his adolescent self proves detrimental. The noncomprehension of a child can be fascinating, but a young adult involved in political activities who falls into a depression that nearly leads to suicide should have something to say about his motives. The lack of introspection leaves a void at the center of *My Universities* and renders it less satisfying than the preceding sections.

Sketches and Fragments

Through Russia (*Po Rusi,* 1912–17), written during a period when Gorky was also hard at work on his autobiography, may be seen as an extension of the trilogy. The inspiration for most of the sketches in the collection comes from events that occurred during Gorky's post-Kazan adventures: his wanderings through southern Russia at the end of the 1880s and through the Caucasus at the beginning of the 1890s. Yet *Through Russia* is quite different. It too is autobiographical, but in a way similar to the earlier stories: that is, the narrator is clearly Gorky, and his own experiences lie behind the works. The focus, however, is not on Alexei Peshkov and his development, but rather on the Russians he meets. It is less the biography of a person than of a land.

The stories of *Through Russia* were composed in two groups. Eleven were originally published in 1912–13 and collected in a volume of 1915 entitled *Through Russia: Sketches* (*Po Rusi: Ocherki*). Eighteen others appeared from late 1915 through 1917.

The working titles for the first group, as well as the way in which Gorky arranged them for the 1915 volume, say much about both the nature of the narrator in these works and Gorky's concept of the collection. In a letter to D. N. Ovsyaniko-Kulikovsky, a prominent philologist and at the time an editor of the journal *Russkii vestnik* [*The Russian Herald*], Gorky said he had intended to subtitle the sketches *Impressions of a Transient*.[21] He specified "transient" (*prokhodiashchii*) and not "passerby" (*prokhozhii*) because he saw the narrator as an active participant and not the passive listener of the earliest stories. Also, the collection includes sketches, notes, and memoirs; the one direct link among them is the individual sensibility of the transient, who travels from one spot to the next. Gorky specifically refers to these pieces as sketches or stories, and not autobiography. He himself expressed some uncertainty about the distinction between a sketch and a story, but he clearly felt that in this collection he was reworking actual events into a literary form. *Through Russia* contains, not reportage, but a personal vision.[22]

That vision is evidenced by his selection of "Birth of a Man" ("Rozhdenie cheloveka," 1912) to open the 1915 volume and "The Deceased" ("Pokoinik," 1912) to close it. Gorky placed the other nine works roughly in the chronological order of the experiences that they reflect, but these two appear out of sequence in order to frame the cycle and perhaps, as has been suggested, to respond to Leonid Andreev's well-known play *The Life of Man* (*Zhizn' cheloveka,* 1907).[23] The opening sketch utilizes an incident of 1892, when Gorky was working on a new highway from Sukhumi to Novorossiisk and came into contact with a group of laborers driven south by the famine that ravaged much of Russia that year. Gorky comes upon a woman with the group who has remained behind to give birth. Serving as midwife, Gorky brings into the world a "new inhabitant of the Russian land, a person of an unknown fate" (14:153). In "The Deceased" Gorky, passing through a tiny settlement, is called upon to read the service for a person who has just died, in the course of which he is interrupted by a drunken deacon the dead man had helped. The next morning Gorky sets out again, leaving behind the corpse and the sleeping deacon. Both works contrast sparks of goodness—the birth of a child, the good deed of the deceased—with the unpleasant surroundings and difficult lives of the people who populate them. This theme, defined so starkly in the framing stories, runs through the entire collection. The possibility, even occasionally the reality of something good, or at least hope for the future, appears within an otherwise dreary setting.[24] The transient narrator, apart from and yet also involved with those whose lives he briefly touches, throws this contrast into relief.

In their melding of understated narrative with violent incident several of the pieces in *Through Russia* are minor masterpieces. Probably its best-known work is "Hobgoblins" (" 'Strasti-mordasti'," 1913, published 1917; also translated as "Lullaby" and "The Creepy-Crawlies"). Even though the story occasionally borders on the maudlin, it depicts more profoundly than any other in the book the coexistence of goodness and ugliness. The narrator helps a drunken woman get home and there meets her young son, a cripple, who keeps a menagerie of insects. The narrator returns the next day to visit the boy, Lenka, bringing him some butterflies and beetles for his collection. He also tells Lenka about the open fields beyond the town, fields Lenka has never seen. At first all is squalid: the crippled boy whose legs are covered by filthy rags; his pathetic collection of insects; the drunken mother, a prostitute whose face is ravaged by syphilis. Both the boy and his mother, though, have some fine qualities. Lenka dreams of the open fields and shows an almost paternal concern for his mother; she in turn genuinely loves her son. In gratitude for the joy he has brought to Lenka, she offers the narrator the only thing she has—herself. The story perhaps shows why Gorky was unwilling to condemn the wrongs he describes elsewhere in *Through Russia*: a closer look may reveal elements of goodness in even the most unpromising people and situations.

Fragments from a Diary: Memoirs (*Zametki iz dnevnika: Vospominan-iia*, 1923–24) belongs chronologically with the works discussed in the next chapter, but in both content and manner the collection is part of Gorky's autobiographical writings. In the trilogy and in *Through Russia* individual scenes and events fit into the whole like parts of a mosaic. Gorky carries that technique to an extreme in these "fragments" (literally "notes" or "jottings"). Single fragments may contain two or more loosely related descriptions of characters, and different sections sometimes hardly seem to come from the same work (the English volume based on this collection, called *Fragments from My Diary* [1924], often splits single fragments from the original into two or more pieces). This disjointedness imparts a highly experimental quality to the collection and recalls some of the modernist techniques favored by Gorky's younger contemporaries.[25]

The fragments cover a large period of Gorky's life. The earliest items go back to the decade beginning around the mid-1890s, and thus form a rough sequel to *Through Russia;* the latter parts deal with the First World War and the onset of revolution. In his conclusion Gorky once again speaks of "truth," saying that many truths are best not recalled, especially those that only degrade people. Yet the collection describes much that is cruel in Russian life. To explain this seeming contradiction, we may note that Gorky considered calling the volume "A Book of the Russian People As They Were":

by showing all that was wrong with the past, he hoped to point the way toward a better future. Thus "The Town" ("Gorodok") describes the people he met when forced to live in Arzamas in 1902. One is the owner of a felt factory who has been reading Nikolai Karamzin's *History of the Russian State* for over three years, has reached the ninth volume, and speaks about it rhapsodically. At the same time, however, he also invites friends over to look through binoculars at a neighboring house, where they can see a doctor and his mistress making love. Another is the watchmaker Kortsov, who boasts of all things Russian, composes and sings absurd verses, speaks lyrically of the polluted townscape, and has invented a lock that will fire a bullet at anyone who tries to put a key into it. Some figures are simply ominous: the hero of "The Penmanship Teacher" ("Uchitel' chistopisaniia") kept a diary, discovered by a new lodger in his rooms, that reveals that this seemingly quiet individual was in fact a cold-blooded murderer. An executioner in "The Hangman" ("Palach") enjoys a feeling of self-importance thanks to his occupation, but he also suffers from nerves and eventually dies in a fall. Gorky's goal in this work is perhaps the opposite of that in *Through Russia*, where an unprepossessing surface may mask good qualities: here the surface appears ordinary, occasionally even attractive, but beneath it lurk the contradictoriness and backwardness of life in the old Russia.

The final sketches, dealing with war and revolution, are more journalistic, but certain passages rise above mere reportage. Under the title "About War and Revolution" ("O voine i revoliutsii") Gorky described incidents that reveal the extent of Russian anti-Semitism; equally memorable in another tale is his description of a longtime revolutionary who feels alienated now that he has reached his goal.

At the end of his *Fragments from a Diary* Gorky quotes a statement by William James, whom he had met when he was in the United States in 1906. James had difficulty in comprehending the Russian people, for, he said, they "seem to be creatures for whom reality is unnecessary, unlawful, or even immoral" (17:229–30). In these wide-ranging notes, sketches, and memoirs Gorky captures that eerie sense of Russian unreality. Although neither *Through Russia* nor *Fragments from a Diary* has received extensive critical attention, each contains many rewarding pages.

Literary Memoirs

Gorky's memoirs and autobiographical writings are among his finest achievements. His writing in the two genres shows structural similarities in its fragmentation and chronological disjunction. Nonetheless, upon close examination all the memoirs reveal an inner logic. Gorky's seemingly casual accumulation of detail enables him to provide a fresh, sometimes startling, and always highly perceptive view of the individual he is describing.

The memoirs include portrayals of a few political figures, in particular Lenin, and also of miscellaneous individuals from Gorky's past, such as the Nizhny Novgorod merchant Nikolai Bogrov. Most notable, though, are his sketches of writers: Lev Tolstoy, Anton Chekhov, Vladimir Korolenko, Leonid Andreev, Alexander Blok, and Sergei Esenin, among others. An element of surprise enters somehow into all the accounts, and we do not know precisely what Gorky wants us to take away from each memoir until the very end. For instance, "Leonid Andreev" (1919), was written (like most of Gorky's recollections devoted to individuals) largely under the influence of feelings engendered by the subject's death. Although Andreev was only slightly younger than Gorky and began publishing just a few years later, Gorky's relationship to him was that of a master to his pupil,[26] in an inversion of the Gorky-Tolstoy relationship where Gorky was the pupil. If Gorky often resented Tolstoy's domineering manner, he was equally resentful of Andreev's unwillingness to follow Gorky's guidance. Gorky took note of a story published in 1898 by the then neophyte writer, and the two men began a close association. Disagreements soon arose, however, and by 1905 the two had already drifted apart. In the last few years of Andreev's life the break was almost total. Gorky finds Andreev the man a wonderful raconteur with a great sense of humor, but he misses that humor in his stories. He is baffled by Andreev's apparent dislike of reading and his careless, almost hostile attitude toward books. Andreev also strikes him as too interested in himself, too aware of the impression he makes both in person and through his works. Furthermore, Andreev's deeply pessimistic outlook on life diverged radically from Gorky's (16:325–26), and was no doubt partly responsible for the differences between them. Elsewhere, most notably in his final novel *The Life of Klim Samgin*, Gorky again depicted Andreev in unflattering terms.[27] This memoir contains more of a chronologically ordered narrative than is usual for Gorky, and it seems to develop in a relatively straightforward way. Yet at the end there is a strange twist. After sketching a scene showing Andreev at his worst (he frightens his little son with a story about death), Gorky suddenly shifts direction. The incident with his son occurs shortly after the death of Andreev's wife. He is visiting Gorky on Capri, where despite his depression he displays an admirable enthusiasm for his writing. Though he offers some further criticism of Andreev's works, from that point on Gorky emphasizes the moments of genuine feeling and even passion in Andreev. Almost despite himself, Gorky leaves his readers with a far more favorable impression of Andreev than they would expect from the bulk of the memoir.

"Anton Chekhov" was written in two parts: one done immediately after Chekhov's death in 1904; the other in 1923. Yet the transition from one section to the next is remarkably smooth, partly because the whole is a series of anecdotes. Gorky introduces seemingly trivial incidents even as he consistently avoids describing major events.[28] For instance, he recalls a visit to Chekhov by a teacher, who immediately begins to pontificate on pedagogical matters. Chekhov disarms him with a simple question about the beating of schoolchildren in his district, and the teacher starts to talk naturally and interestingly. Something similar occurs during a visit by three women who feel they must discuss the war between the Greeks and the Turks, but Chekhov quickly turns their attention to jam, a topic about which they can speak knowledgeably. At the end several brief scenes describe Chekhov's attitudes toward Tolstoy, whose failings he understands yet whom he treats affectionately. In this sketch, as in that on Tolstoy, an image emerges through the accumulation of detail. The surprise is not in the ending, but in the way a handful of apparently random moments can reveal so much about a man. This brief and fragmentary memoir presents a more memorable picture of the man than many a full-length study.

Gorky's memoir of Tolstoy is most surprising in its very form. The first part contains forty-four "notes" of varying length written for the most part in 1901–2, when the two writers met regularly in the Crimea. The second half consists of a long letter written immediately after Tolstoy's death in 1910. Many of the points made in the notes are repeated or embellished in the letter, for Gorky made no effort to edit the two disparate sections. In a sense, however, the entire work was "composed" in 1919: the critic Viktor Shklovsky recalls having seen the work in manuscript and indicates that Gorky carefully rearranged (and presumably even edited) the notes in order to create the effect he desired.[29] Once again the result is a mosaic, but here the pieces seem chosen and arranged more arbitrarily than is the case with the Chekhov memoir. In any case, it is immediately obvious that the forty-four notes provide revealing insights: "[Tolstoy] always speaks about Buddhism and Christ sentimentally, and about Christ especially badly—with no enthusiasm or pathos in his words and not a single spark of fire in his heart. I think that he considers Christ to be naive, worthy of pity. Though at times he admires him, he hardly loves him. And he seems to be afraid that if Christ were to come to a Russian village the girls would laugh at him" (16:264). It soon becomes clear that these passages are no collection of mere random jottings at all; rather, themes coalesce, and with them emerges a terribly complex figure, a person far harder to comprehend—or like—than Chekhov.

Gorky's feelings about Tolstoy were ambiguous even before they met; in his earliest stories he quarrels with the philosophy of living known as Tolstoyanism.[30] The memoir itself might be viewed as an effort to separate, or perhaps "save," Tolstoy the writer from Tolstoy the publicist.[31] The emphasis is on concrete detail, on dialogue, on observed incident: in the notes, and even in the letter, Gorky largely avoids abstract generalization. Tolstoy turns out to be physically less imposing than we might expect and yet he is a towering spiritual presence. If he pities Christ, that may be because he regards God as a more worthy equal. The entire question of Tolstoy's attitude toward religion is one of the memoir's dominant motifs. Then there is the relationship between Gorky and Tolstoy. Gorky often feels bullied by Tolstoy, who could behave quite crudely. He tormented Gorky with direct and sometimes embarrassing questions, offered blunt and cutting criticism, and spoke disparagingly about women. But Gorky by no means dwells on the negative. For instance, several of the notes carefully follow Tolstoy's thought processes, showing how he would seize upon an idea, develop it, and then move off in new directions.[32] The final portrait is striking in its searing honesty and uncompromising complexity. Gorky shows that genius is not the same as sainthood, that the closer one comes to greatness the more elusive a full understanding of it becomes.

Chapter Six

Final Achievements

Master of the Short Form

The last decade and a half of Gorky's career was a time of fervid activity, yet the number of titles he completed then is small if compared to, say, his publications during the first fifteen years of the century. From the 1920s on he wrote some of the autobiographical works and memoirs discussed in the preceding chapter, but he published only a handful of stories, two novels, and three plays. But this seeming decline in productivity is partly deceptive. One of the novels, *The Life of Klim Samgin,* is by far the largest work he ever wrote, and occupied much of his time during his final years. During the 1930s, when his work on the novel slowed, Gorky's journalism consumed a large percentage of his creative time. In fact Gorky had less and less time to write at all. His trips to the Soviet Union in the late 1920s and early 1930s occasioned long interruptions in his work. His health, never robust, troubled him at intervals. Still, even if his literary output declined in quantity, he produced several fine works and explored new directions. In its scale as well as its encyclopedic character *The Life of Klim Samgin* represented a bold experiment, and his later plays, while similar to his earlier work, consciously embrace revolutionary themes.

Gorky's willingness to experiment is most evident in his *Stories of 1922–1924 (Rasskazy 1922–1924 godov).* Several of these nine stories recall the Gorky of the shorter works dating back to the 1890s in which the narrator meets a figure who in turn relates a tale of his own. The stories of the 1920s differ in that Gorky reduces his own role; he largely avoids the philosophizing and authorial asides that guided the reader in his earlier fiction and often robbed it of subtlety. The voice and nature of the story's main character determine the style and atmosphere of the entire work. Since the narrator does not pass judgment, Gorky's own position is more difficult to detect. The result recalls the *skaz* technique perfected

by Nikolai Leskov: the highly distinctive voice of a character replaces
that of an author, whose own outlook is concealed.[1]

At times Gorky's subject matter is as new as his narrative technique. For instance, "The Story of a Novel" ("Rasskaz ob odnom
romane," 1922–23) describes a woman who meets a character from
a novel being written by an author she knows. It would be easy to
dismiss the incident as a hallucination, but that would be to mis-
interpret the story. Gorky is openly parodying the clichés of literary
love at the same time that he willfully confuses the real and the
unreal. At bottom the tale is an attack on convention. The character
the woman meets is too artificial; in a real-life situation he is simply
inadequate. The novelist destroys his partly written novel at the
end, thus showing that he recognizes his failure. By implication
Gorky urges writers to avoid the familiar, to test out new forms
and new subject matter.[2]

His efforts to find a fresh approach are evident in "The Hermit"
("Otshel'nik," 1922), the work that opens the collection. The title
figure, Savel Pilshchik (Savel the Sawyer), had been accused many
years earlier of having an affair with his daughter. Though there
apparently really was something between them, he was acquitted
and then left his hometown. He later tries to locate his daughter,
only to learn that she has since died. After further wandering he
arrives at a place by the river Oka and ministers to the people who
come to him for advice, offering others consolation rather in the
manner of Luka from *The Lower Depths*. Savel tells his life story to
the narrator, who on subsequent occasions watches him giving advice
to those who visit him. In outline the format resembles those found
in Gorky's earlier stories. But there are two crucial differences. First,
the narrator does not condemn Savel's "consoling lies," but instead
leaves any conclusions about him up to the reader.[3] The narrator's
final remark is phrased as a question, not a statement: "Is this a
holy man who possesses the treasure of unlimited love for the world?"
(17:260). Throughout the narrator does not interject his own views
but merely observes. And this leads to the second distinguishing
characteristic: it is difficult to associate the narrator with Gorky
himself. The author's voice is so muted that the stories are seemingly
more "objective" than is usually the case in his works.

In "A Sky-Blue Life" ("Golubaia zhizn'," 1924), the subject is
madness. Konstantin Mironov, whose somewhat distracted father
and overbearing mother have died, is slowly losing contact with

reality. At first he simply compares the life around him unfavorably with the Paris of his imagination. Then he is so taken by the shade light (sky) blue that he decides to have his house painted that color. He is tormented more and more by the unwelcome attentions of a carpenter, a character the writer Mikhail Prishvin once described as a devil figure.[4] This time the narrator appears only at the conclusion when it transpires that a doctor's account of Mironov's illness has formed the basis for everything up to that point. The narrator then goes off to find Mironov, who has been cured for some time and now works as a bookbinder. The carpenter is long dead, as is a woman Mironov had courted during his illness and later married. The cured Mironov turns out to be quite dull. The irony of the ending is that he was in some ways more attractive when mad. Earlier Gorky skillfully depicts Mironov's rapid descent from eccentricity into insanity; Konstantin becomes more and more suspicious and less able to cope with the disruptions brought about by the carpenter. The latter in turn veers from the boisterous to the diabolical; it is never clear to what extent the carpenter simply acts out of a combination of impudence and a dull-witted insensitivity, or whether he is indeed a dark force. The reader is adrift, viewing the action through Mironov's perceptions, which are not at first sufficiently crazed to serve as a warning. The ambiguity and psychological perceptiveness of "A Sky-Blue Life" distinguish it from most of what Gorky had written before.

The stories from the collection discussed so far are notable in that, although written after the revolution, they are essentially apolitical. In several works, though, Gorky explores the reactions of individuals to the upheavals of the revolution. "Karamora" (1923) represents, as Gorky himself declared, an effort to depict a traitor to the revolutionary cause who emerges even worse than the notorious double agent Azev.[5] Pyotr Karazin, the first-person narrator, tells his story while in prison. Nicknamed Karamora by his father, he at first had been an enthusiastic supporter of the revolution. As a result of his political activities he had been arrested more than once. Then one day he yields to the urgings of a police official and agrees to become a double agent. From then on he betrays his comrades regularly, though, as he also notes, at times he would help revolutionaries escape from prison or exile without the knowledge of those for whom he was supposedly working. Karamora is both stronger and more complex than Gorky's other police spies.

He does not work for the police out of cowardice, but rather because
of a profound internal emptiness. He lacks a sense of self and believes
that at least two quite different people live inside him—and perhaps
three and even four (17:372).[6] His inability to choose a personality
corresponds to his indifference to good and evil,[7] so that his "rebellion" against the revolution occurs more by chance than by conviction. In his potential for evil and his inner void Karamora recalls
several of Dostoevsky's characters—Svidrigailov (*Crime and Punishment*) or Stavrogin and to a lesser degree Pyotr Verkhovensky (both
from *The Possessed*). This story, perhaps more than any other, shows
that Gorky, despite his conscious rejection of Dostoevsky's views,
was nonetheless fascinated by some of the problems his great predecessor raised and was not averse to dealing with them in his own
way.

In all, the *Stories of 1922–1924* show that even the mature Gorky
was constantly searching, always willing to try new forms and new
themes. In these works he seems more prepared to let his characters
and their actions speak for themselves, a sign of confidence in his
own abilities. Of most significance, though, are Gorky's attempts
at psychological exploration. In these stories external events and
often the political background are still important, but here Gorky
probes his characters more deeply and raises questions not always
easily resolved. Consequently these pieces are more ambiguous and
complex than his earlier work.

Last Plays

After completing work on *The Old Man*, apparently by 1917,
Gorky, then one of the most widely performed playwrights in Russia, seemed to lose interest in the dramatic form. The full-length
Yakov Bogomolov, on which he worked in 1916 and perhaps later,
remained only a draft. During the 1920s he wrote a few film scen-
arios, which were not immediately published. His one major project
in this genre at that time appears to have been his reworking of *The
Counterfeit Coin*.

Only in 1930 did Gorky return to play-writing and then he
worked on two plays simultaneously. Of these, *Somov and Others*
(*Somov i drugie*, 1931) was sent to Berlin for possible staging, but
in the end it remained both unpublished and unperformed during
Gorky's lifetime. While not one of his better efforts, it represents

a novel attempt of Gorky's to deal with a contemporary postrevolutionary theme: the so-called "wreckers," engineers and others who were supposedly undermining the Soviet Union's effort to industrialize. The show trials that began in 1928, precursors of the "Great Terror" of a few years later, gave Gorky the idea for this play. Written as an exposé of the types of individuals involved in the "wrecking," ending with the arrest of Somov and the "others," the play makes painful reading today in the light of history. Surprisingly, Somov and his acquaintances, the villains of the piece, spend so much time on stage that several—Somov, and particularly Yaropegov, an old school chum of his—acquire a certain depth and even grandeur as individuals. The heroes, the true Bolsheviks, by contrast remain shadowy and ill defined.[8]

Gorky's other play of that time became an important part of his dramatic legacy: *Egor Bulychov and Others* (*Egor Bulychov i drugie*, 1932), the first of the three full-length plays that Gorky completed at the end of his life. As in many of Gorky's plays, its most notable feature is its strong but contradictory central figure, Egor Bulychov, who recalls the merchants from the plays of the 1910s, such as Antipa Zykov and the "old man," Mastakov.[9] The setting is again a large provincial town. Bulychov has lived solely for his work, and by the standards of his day is a success. True, he has also been grasping and ruthless, a person never influenced by moral considerations. Despite his misdeeds, Bulychov still displays a certain majesty. Unlike many of his fellow merchants, he has at least been direct in getting what he wants, and that through inner strength and sheer work. The play describes him at a time of crisis. On the one hand, he is terminally ill with cancer of the liver. He is reluctant to accept both the reality and the finality of his illness, but his increasing frailty reminds him that he must deal with the inevitable, and he begins to question the values by which he had lived. The other part of his crisis is more social and political. The fateful year 1917 arrives, and with it the impending collapse of the old order. There are many references to these upheavals: wounded soldiers return from the front, the tsar abdicates, workers' movements are spreading. Those in Bulychov's class scramble to retain what they have. For his part Bulychov, as he questions his own past, also questions the actions of the government and of society. What gives Bulychov grandeur are his recognition that his life has been wrong and his sympathy with those who want to change society. In his last months he does not sink into despair, but rather attains a new level of insight.

Little actually happens during the play's three acts. It has often been said that Bulychov's death represents the end of the old order, but he does not so much die along with it as foretell its departure. He is impatient with his wife, Ksenya, who wants things to continue as they are, and strongly opposed to their daughter, Varvara, who along with her husband, Zvontsov, is busily working to obtain the inheritance. Bulychov also has little regard for his fellow merchants: the machinations of old acquaintances such as Bashkin and Dostigaev no longer interest him. The play has few positive characters other than Bulychov and his illegitimate daughter, Shura. Yakov Laptev, Bulychov's godson, is clearly a revolutionary, but he is a relatively minor figure—indeed, the bulk of his part was written into the play when it was already in rehearsal. [10] Bulychov cares less about the nature of the future society than he does about rejecting the one he has known. In his scenes with the abbess Melania (his wife's sister) and with the priest Pavlin (who wants Bulychov to contribute toward a bell for his church), Bulychov offers cutting comments on both organized religion and the tsarist government. While family intrigues proceed with intense seriousness, his mocking sallies provide an element of humor that keeps the play from becoming overly gloomy. [11] Over the last half of the play a mad, at times grotesquely comic, whirlwind symbolizes the general decline. At the end of act 2 Bulychov is introduced to a fireman who plays the trumpet and is convinced that the blasts on his instrument can cure people. The amateur musician, not accidentally named Gavrilo (Gabriel), begins to blow his trumpet, and Bulychov declares that he is announcing the end of the world. In the third act a sorceress and a "holy fool" visit Bulychov, with Melania's encouragement, to help cure him. Against the background of conniving by Bulychov's family and business associates, the discordant interruptions created by these half-crazed visitors symbolize the chaos into which all Russia is falling. As the play ends, the mortally ill Bulychov hears the strains of a revolutionary song outside his window. It is too late for him, but a new order approaches.

Gorky's next play, *Dostigaev and Others* (*Dostigaev i drugie*, 1933), is a direct sequel to *Egor Bulychov and Others*. Set during the months after Bulychov's death, it traces the fate of many characters from the earlier work up to the 1917 revolution. The title figure, a minor character in the first play, resembles Bulychov: both have been ruthless businessmen, both fully comprehend the corruption of the society in which they live. There is an important difference, however: Dostigaev is more cynical. The sympathy he expresses for the revolution arises not, as in Bulychov's case, from new insight, but out of opportunism: his basic outlook has not changed.[12] He and his wife join a demonstration at the end of *Egor Bulychov* because they understand that sympathy for workers' movements is now in vogue. In this play Dostigaev recognizes that the revolutionaries are about to take power, and he tries to maintain ties with them without breaking his links with more conservative forces. His middle way leads nowhere. At the end his daughter has committed suicide, while Dostigaev and the rest of his family are under arrest.

Even though *Dostigaev* shares a number of characters and its setting with *Egor Bulychov*, it is a quite different work. *Dostigaev* contains far more characters, with much heavier representation of both reactionary and revolutionary forces. Among the latter, Yakov Laptev appears again, but he is partly overshadowed by new characters. Also, whereas the action of *Egor Bulychov* is confined to Bulychov's home, here each act takes place in a different location—first at a merchants' club, then in the Bulychov house, and finally at Dostigaev's home.[13] It is not just the settings that vary: in each of the three acts the nature of the action changes, and, except for Dostigaev himself, no major character appears throughout the play. Two thirds of the cast appear in only a single act.[14] Act 1 concentrates on the merchants and their dread of revolution; act 2 focuses more on the revolution and on those who are part of, or at least sympathetic to, the movement; act 3 portrays the defeat of Dostigaev and the forces associated with him. If the play has a fault, it lies in Dostigaev. His cynicism soon wears thin, and in any case he is rather peripheral to what is going on. The play thus lack a strong center.

Gorky's final play, *Vassa Zheleznova*, was a total revision of a play originally written in 1910. It had been frequently staged in the meantime, but in preparation for a new staging he was asked to "update" it to reflect contemporary themes. Gorky, however, did not confine himself to minor changes. Vassa Zheleznova herself remains much the same, albeit her new patronymic—Borisovna instead of Petrovna—indicates that even she is different in some way. Gorky did his primary work on the new version at the very end of 1935, and it premiered the following summer, a few weeks after his death.

To appreciate Gorky's final dramatic work we must say a few words about the original version, which was subtitled *Mother*. Written just before the series of plays (*The Counterfeit Coin*, *The Zykovs*, *The Old Man*) that comprised some of Gorky's best work, the 1910 *Vassa Zheleznova* shares many traits with them. The plot is fairly straightforward, centering on the struggle over the inheritance of Zakhar Zheleznov, who during the first two acts is slowly dying offstage. Vassa, his wife, has helped her husband build up their business, and now plots cunningly with the firm's manager, Mikhail, to gain control of the money. The business would normally be inherited by her two sons: Pavel, a cripple married to Mikhail's daughter Lyudmila; and Semyon, married to the greedy Natalya. Vassa's daughter Anna, who is married to an officer and lives in another town, returns home upon hearing of her father's illness. Also living in the house is Prokhor, Zakhar's dissolute brother, who has invested in the business and has eyes on the money himself. The tensions among these rivals frequently erupt into open conflict, with first one and then another gaining the upper hand. During one argument Pavel gets into a fight with Prokhor, who suffers a heart attack and dies. Pavel and Semyon, along with Natalya, claim the inheritance as theirs, but Mikhail and Vassa then produce a will of Zakhar's leaving everything to his wife. Vassa sends Pavel off to a monastery, drives Semyon and Natalya away, and finally promises her support to Anna and Lyudmila.

The play's power again depends upon its title character. Like other merchants in Gorky's work of the time, she has good sides that mitigate her less attractive qualities. The subtitle *Mother*, which recalls Gorky's novel of the same name, indicates that for all her rapacity she can be protective toward those she loves. Her desire to take control of the business arises from a genuine wish to prevent her incompetent sons from destroying what she and her husband have built up over the years. At the end of the play she offers help to those she truly loves: she urges her daughter to leave her drunken husband and bring her children, and she promises Lyudmila a dowry when she finds a new husband. They in turn exclaim at the miracles she has seemingly wrought. Vassa rejects that attitude: "There are no miracles for us . . . . None! We must do everything ourselves"

(13:232). Her entire life has been a struggle, and by now she finds herself hearing voices—she will no longer know any peace. The conflicting qualities within her raise Vassa to the stature of a tragic figure. She is guilty of much wrong, but often she was inspired by a desire for the good. At the final curtain the three women share the stage—Vassa, with her wealth intact; Lyudmila, freed from her marriage and starting life anew; and Anna, also looking forward to a fresh start. The men, except for Mikhail, are dissolute and weak; Vassa's masculine rivals are either dead or in retreat. Perhaps nowhere else in Gorky's work do the women rout the men so completely.

The 1935 play removes the contradictions from Vassa's character. She is involved with a much larger business, a steamship company, and her whole life is centered upon it and her other possessions. No longer so concerned with her role as a "mother," she largely ignores her children.[15] The revised Vassa is a clearer archetype of the aggressive, nouveau riche merchant in prerevolutionary Russia and an effective character, but is less a tragic figure than an embodiment of evil. As a result the reworked play lacks the psychological depth of the earlier version. This Vassa too has a confidante, a woman named Anna, who helps her with her various schemes. The character Prokhor reappears, though now he is Vassa's brother rather than her husband's. She has two teenage daughters living at home and a son abroad in political exile. The inheritance battle is still important, but in trying to make his play more relevant to the 1930s Gorky placed greater emphasis on the depravity of the ruling class and introduced references to politics.

The theme of depravity comes out most clearly in the greatly changed character of Vassa's husband, here called Sergei. He has been accused of seducing children, and his effort to cover up his crimes by bribery has failed. Vassa insists that he take poison in order to save the family from possibly ruinous scandal. When he resists, she threatens to reveal even more about his crimes, and the first act ends with his death. Prokhor, whose role in this version has been expanded, is if anything even more dissolute than before: he seems interested in every woman he encounters, including his own nieces. Political issues emerge most clearly through Vassa's daughter-in-law Rachel, who returns from abroad in act 2 to inform Vassa that her son Fyodor is dying. Rachel wants to retrieve her own son, whom she had left with Vassa when Rachel and Fyodor fled Russia. But Vassa will not give up her only grandchild, whom she is keeping some miles away and raising to inherit the steamship company. In act 3 the two argue over political issues, and Vassa decides to hand Rachel over to the police. That evening, though, Vassa abruptly dies, and as the play ends, Anna and Prokhor are vying to steal what they can.

Vassa lacks the self-awareness of an Egor Bulychov, who foresees the end of his world: she seems to believe her way of life will continue forever.[16] Though poorly motivated dramatically, her death symbolizes the abruptness with which established society can (and will) collapse. At the end her younger daughter Lyudmila, who verges on being simpleminded and has been brusquely ignored by her mother earlier, is the only person to show any grief at Vassa's death.

Vassa Zheleznova, while not among Gorky's best dramatic work, nonetheless contains one of his towering central characters. Through Vassa and her sudden downfall at the very moment of her triumph Gorky tellingly conveys both her inner fragility and that of the society she represents.

Toward the Epic

Gorky's final two novels develop the tendency already evident in *The Life of Matvei Kozhemiakin*—the attempt to depict the historical changes in Russia over the latter part of the nineteenth century and the early part of the twentieth through the story of a single family or individual. In that novel, however, these events provide only a faint background echo. They play a more important role in *The Artamonov Business*, and in Gorky's last novel, *The Life of Klim Samgin*, they are described directly.

Although a decade and a half separate the publication of *The Life of Matvei Kozhemiakin* from that of *The Artamonov Business* (*Delo Artamonovykh*, 1924–25), Gorky had conceived the rough idea for his penultimate novel as early as 1904, and during 1916 and 1917 he had worked on a manuscript tentatively titled *The Atamanovs* (*Atamanovy*).[17] In other words, for at least two decades Gorky had toyed with the idea of a novel that would present a vast panorama of Russian life over at least two generations. *The Artamonov Business* spans a lengthy period, from 1863 up to the revolution, and yet it is almost classical in its construction, following the fortunes of a single family and largely confined to a single setting.

The founder of the book's short-lived dynasty, Ilya Artamonov, is one of Gorky's larger-than-life figures. A former serf, he has worked as the steward on an estate. He arrives in the town of Dryomov ("Sleepyville") determined to build his own mill. With him are three sons: Pyotr, the eldest, who soon becomes the work's most important figure; Nikita, a hunchback; and Alexei, actually an adopted nephew. The townspeople, accustomed to their slow, backward way of life, regard the energetic Ilya with a mixture of curiosity and quiet hostility. The linen mill that he rapidly builds and expands is not so much a part of the town as something carved out of it. He combines strength and determination with cruelty and greed. But his dynasty is doomed by his inability to pass on to others the positive qualities that enabled him to succeed.

Pyotr, who is destined to take over the factory, turns out to be indecisive. Although the mill prospers under him, he feels that it owns him rather than he it. As time goes on he develops a split personality; his second self is an "injured" man who confronts the first Pyotr with both his guilt and his sense of a wasted life. Pyotr fights with his double, but at the same time has need of him: "The injured man was pleasantly necessary for Artamonov senior, like a steam bath attendant who rubs the soft, well-soaped, and pleasantly hot piece of bast on just that part of a man's back that he cannot reach himself" (18:294–95). Pyotr's double, then, is not so much an opponent as a necessary invention to ease the split between what he is and what he should have been.[18] He creates a better but safely nonexistent self. In his daily life Pyotr becomes more alienated from others: from his wife, whom he married mostly because of his father, from his children; and from the world outside Dryomov, which is undergoing changes that ultimately destroy both him and his factory.

Ilya's other children fare no better. The hunchback Nikita spends much of his life in a monastery, where he attains local renown and is actively sought out by pilgrims. As in *A Confession*, Gorky depicts monastery life as no more spiritual—and in some ways even more material—than secular life. Nikita finally returns home to die. Alexei, the adopted brother, is in certain ways a counterpoint to Pyotr. While Pyotr is quite uninterested in political and social issues, Alexei becomes totally absorbed in them from a liberal standpoint like that of Zakhar and Polina Bardin in the play *Enemies*. And like them he too is helpless before the onrush of events. Alexei dies naturally but totally unexpectedly, as though cast aside by fate. Nor does the younger generation do well. Miron, Alexei's son, takes a serious interest in the business, but he is no more able to control events than his father. If Pyotr is a weaker version of his father, then Pyotr's son Yakov represents a further enfeeblement of the line. Yakov, from whose viewpoint much of the novel's last section is presented, perishes while attempting to escape from the disturbances accompanying the onset of revolution.

The novel avoids certain formulas common in Gorky's earlier novels. While Pyotr is undoubtedly the most important single figure, he does not dominate from beginning to end in the manner of Foma Gordeev or Matvei Kozhemiakin. Gorky omits the bildungsroman portion of the work and introduces Pyotr as a young adult. At the very beginning Pyotr is overshadowed by his father; later he yields to Yakov. He cannot control his destiny or even understand the social and historical forces that threaten his world. If the book has a central figure, it is the factory, whose "life story" is told from its birth in the opening chapters until its death after the revolution. Moreover, the business as it were devours the Artamonovs. Ilya dies while helping move a boiler into the plant; Pyotr feels that the factory is either out of control or that it controls him, while his brother Alexei and the offspring of both are totally taken up with it.

Gorky says little about 1917 itself and its aftermath; his late works tend to end rather than begin with the October Revolution. But here the gathering storm has a more definite form than it did in Gorky's earlier writings. The main revolutionary figure is Pyotr's older son Ilya, who breaks with his father and from then on appears in the book only in scattered references. In a draft version of the novel Gorky described Ilya's return just as the revolutionary forces were taking over,[19] but omitted the entire passage from the final version, and with good reason: the Artamonov business had long existed in isolation from the rest of Dryomov, to say nothing of the outside world. The new social forces, which do have an effect on the factory, remain vague and mysterious to Pyotr and Yakov. Introducing Ilya at the very end would have dissipated the uncertain atmosphere that Gorky had created.

Indeed, despite the looming presence of the revolution, the rustic, almost primeval setting and the emphasis on the more distant past predominate in *The Artamonov Business*. In a letter to Gorky Konstantin Fedin noted that the novel struck him as out of balance; about half of it deals with only seven years (roughly 1863 to 1870), while the second half races through the forty-seven years remaining until the revolution.[20] Indeed, the novel's most prophetic voice, like the novel itself, seems to have difficulty in separating himself from mid-century. Tikhon Vyalov, no longer young even at the novel's beginning, at various times stands as the Artamonovs' accuser and becomes the inspiration for the younger Ilya's apostasy. As the story unfolds, Tikhon ages more slowly than the Artamonovs: he would have to be 90 or 100 by its end, and yet he seems much younger.[21] Gorky evidently uses Tikhon primarily as a symbol: as a person close to the land who maintains his ties to the common folk, he embodies their call for vengeance. Although he could be interpreted as a harbinger of the factory's destruction, he is less a representative of the revolution himself than a voice—perhaps even the spirit—of the rural Russia that seeks to repel the intrusions of the Artamonovs and their ilk.

The Life of Klim Samgin: Forty Years (*Zhizn' Klima Samgina: Sorok let*, 1925–36) was not merely Gorky's last novel, but a massive unfinished epic that occupied the last dozen years of his life. As with *The Artamonov Business*, Gorky intended to end the work roughly at 1917, but it essentially deals with the preceding "forty years." The protagonist, Klim Samgin, shares several traits with the main figures of Gorky's prerevolutionary novels. He encounters opportunities for success, but turns out to be a person of only average abilities who makes a series of wrong turns in life. With time— and, of course, after Gorky's canonization as a classic of Soviet literature—the novel has come to be recognized, at least in official Soviet critical circles, as Gorky's masterpiece. At the same time western critics have remained distinctly cool toward the work, often considering it decidedly inferior to *The Artamonov Business*. Typical is the comment of Gleb Struve: "With its multitude of characters and its extremely uninteresting hero, it is diffuse and dull, and it reveals glaringly Gorky's lack of constructive ability."[22]

Struve's specific points, albeit not his overall rejection of the novel, undergird much of the comment made on it even in the Soviet Union. Those who admire the novel still find it necessary to defend Gorky's choice of a hero, its seemingly random construction, and its sheer range of material. As the writer Alexei Chapygin noted in a letter to Gorky, the historical background, while presented effectively, occasionally threatens to overwhelm the work.[23] The novel is huge—some twenty-two hundred pages and four volumes

in the authoritative Soviet edition of Gorky. Along with the me-
ticulous historical detail Chapygin mentions, it contains an enormous number of characters, many of whom appear and disappear
at odd intervals. A few critics, though, have esteemed it for its very
complexity: Boris Pasternak preferred the first part of *The Life of
Klim Samgin* to *The Artamonov Business* precisely because it required
a greater effort to read and comprehend.[24]

Some of the novel's weaknesses may be traced to the circumstances
under which it was written. The first two volumes were done quickly,
considering their size. Gorky commenced serious work on the project
early in 1925 and finished both some three years later, in February
1928. Volume 3, which incorporates some material originally intended for volume 2 and dating from 1927, was largely written
between 1928 and 1930, with long interruptions occasioned by
Gorky's trips from Italy to the Soviet Union. The fourth part was
composed primarily in the Soviet Union, but Gorky's poor health
and his intense publicistic activity slowed his progress on it. He
eventually realized that it would be necessary to redo at least part
of the novel, but he never found the time. At one point he said,
perhaps exaggeratedly, that he should rewrite the novel from beginning to end.[25] In any case, his decision to pick up the action in
volume 4 at a date *before* the action in volume 3 ends indicates that
he planned to revise volume 3 extensively.[26] And volume 4 itself
was left largely in draft form. No doubt Gorky would have greatly
reworked this volume had he lived, but as it stands it suffers from
rough edges, as does volume 3 to a lesser degree.

The novel is certainly diffuse: it would benefit from a glossary of
historical names and events. Nonetheless, it achieves a degree of
unity both through Klim Samgin and through several secondary
figures who appear throughout. The changing but frequently fascinating cast of auxiliary fictional and real-life characters helps make
the novel engrossing, as do the historical scenes that sometimes
disrupt the narrative. To be sure, the work as a whole is one more
"large loose baggy monster" in the Russian tradition, yet it is less
daunting than it might at first seem.

The novel has a double mission. On the one hand it chronicles
Russia's intellectual and political history from the 1870s until the
revolution. Partly in order to follow the major events of the day,
Gorky constantly shifts the scene of the novel's action: it begins in
the Volga region, but later Klim goes to Saint Petersburg and

Moscow, to other Russian cities, and even abroad—with many trips back and forth among the various locations. Along the way Gorky tells his readers what people were reading and discussing during each period he describes. The second mission is to analyze the psychology of those in the educated urban population who ended up opposing the revolution.[27] Some come from wealthy merchant families; others have had to battle poverty. Within the novel a few people from this class support the revolution, but Gorky concentrates on those who ultimately turn away from it. While he does not probe his heroes so deeply as in some of his short stories from the early 1920s, his goal is to examine the motivations of such individuals.

If the size and intentions of *Klim Samgin* are unusually ambitious, Gorky's hero and the manner of his depiction are familiar enough. Once again Gorky describes a life from beginning to end. (Although it is not absolutely certain that Gorky would have had Samgin die at the end of the novel, the revolution clearly swept away the order to which he belonged.)[28] Klim seems typically promising as a child, but soon lags behind others in a variety of ways. While his peers are frequently caught up in some movement, Samgin seems incapable of total commitment to anything. At certain times—especially during the revolutionary year of 1905—he finds himself physically and even to an extent spiritually on the side of the revolutionaries, but he then lets the cause move on without him. Like Foma Gordeev, Matvei Kozhemiakin, or Pyotr Artamonov, he is fundamentally passive. He does not so much march through life as let himself be carried along by it. His strained relations with his family also recall the situations of Gorky's earlier protagonists. Early in volume 1 Klim's brother Dmitry and his father leave his native Volga town while he and his mother stay behind. His mother remains a distant and somewhat foreboding person to him. While the subject is not broached in detail, Klim seems particularly uncomfortable with her sexuality—the breakup of her marriage is preceded by an open affair with Varavka, whom she later marries. Varavka thus becomes the powerful (step)father figure of the novel, reminiscent of such characters as Ilya Artamonov.[29] Klim has little subsequent contact with his natural father, who spends much time in Europe, although he is present when his father dies in Vyborg. By way of contrast, he comes across his brother several times: Dmitry grows from a fat and unprepossessing child into a young man both more knowledgeable than Klim and committed to the revolutionary cause.

Several of Klim's boyhood acquaintances turn up time and again throughout his life. For instance, Lyubov Somova, who seems no more impresssive than Dmitry as a child, ends up equally committed to the revolution. Lidia Varavka, the daughter of Klim's stepfather from his first marriage, as an adolescent apparently possesses the understanding and direction Klim lacks. Some time later she and Klim have an affair, then they drift apart and finally her life goes astray; unlike her erstwhile friend Lyuba, Lidia abandons revolutionary activity in favor of religious mysticism. These examples point to a feature that distinguishes this novel from much of Gorky's early work: characters, especially those from Samgin's hometown, are capable of changing with the times. The novel contains a handful of clearly virtuous figures—in particular the Marxist Kutuzov, whom Klim first meets when he goes to study in Saint Petersburg—and a few unalterable villains. But the unpredictable changes experienced by the leading characters impart to the novel a sense of the complex variety of actual life.

Gorky regarded Klim Samgin as an antihero. In going from the draft to the published version of volume 1 he was careful to make him less positive.[30] A telling incident occurs early in volume 1, when Klim is skating with Lidia, her brother Boris, and Lyuba's sister. The latter two suddenly fall through the ice. Klim holds out a strap to Boris, who is being pulled under by the frantic efforts of Lyuba's sister. When Klim realizes that they are dragging him into the water he lets go of the strap and the other two drown. Afterward a peasant who happens upon the tragedy during the fruitless search for Boris's body mutters, "But was there really a boy? Maybe there wasn't one" (21:87). These words haunt Klim for the rest of his life. The incident does not so much determine the subsequent course of his life as delineate a fatal flaw in his character: he lacks the selflessness to give of himself to others or to a cause.

Klim Samgin's biography provides the framework for a depiction of the entire epoch. At first Gorky emphasizes the general atmosphere of the 1870s and 1880s; he cites few dates during much of the first volume. Toward the end of that volume he describes the stampede and deaths that occurred during Nicholas II's coronation ceremony in 1896, and from then on regularly mentions major historical events: the Russo-Japanese war, the assassination of various government ministers, and, most of all, the pivotal year 1905. Indeed, 1905, which bridges volumes 2 and 3, serves as the turning point for the novel as well as for Russia. Samgin witnesses the events of 9 January 1905, and he even meets the instigator of that demonstration, Father Gapon. Later that year, in Moscow, since his home is located near one of the barricades set up in the city, he observes violent excesses on both sides. The pages describing 1905 are among the best in the novel; the picture of Samgin wandering about during Bloody Sunday is particularly effective. He knows that something important is going on, but he lacks overall perspective on it as he haphazardly wanders into and out of danger much like Pierre at the Battle of Borodino in Tolstoy's *War and Peace*.

Gorky often used real-life prototypes for his heroes, in many cases individuals his readers at the time could still identify. For instance, Vladimir Lyutov, whose path frequently crosses Klim's, was based on such capitalist supporters of the revolution as Savva Morozov and Savva Mamontov.[31] Samgin himself was probably derived from several individuals, though in his case positive identifications are difficult.[32] In general, the novel's references to literary and cultural figures make it a virtual history of Russian intellectual life during the years before the revolution.[33] Gorky even mentions himself, attributing negative appraisals of his work to various characters, and speaks of *The Lower Depths* several times. The first half of the novel includes frequent mention of writers well-known during Samgin's youth, such as Nikolai Nekrasov and Lev Tolstoy, while in the second half modernists such as Fyodor Sologub and Dmitry Merezhkovsky are discussed. Gorky also refers to writers he disliked: along with Sologub and Merezhkovsky, these include Dostoevsky and also Leonid Andreev, who even appears directly in the novel.

The Life of Klim Samgin is also replete with allusions to the Bible. No doubt many of these are included because they characterize the milieu Gorky describes,[34] and yet there seem to be more than necessary for that purpose alone. Certainly the use of "forty years" in Gorky's subtitle imparts religious overtones to this account of Klim Samgin's wanderings. Thus for all its inchoate action, unlikely coincidences, overnumerous characters, and intimidating bulk, *The Life of Klim Samgin* stands as a noble effort and a bold conclusion to the career of a writer always ready to try something new.

Chapter Seven
Conclusion

In his essay "How I Learned to Write" (1928) Gorky reviewed his career and discovered two complementary sources for his fiction: "I gathered impressions both from life and from books. The first group of impressions can be compared to raw material, the second to a semi-manufactured product."[1] A few pages later he notes: "When retelling the plots of books I had read, I more and more frequently caught myself not retelling them exactly, but distorting what I had read and adding something of my own, based on my own experience. That happened because the facts of life and of literature had melded together for me. A book is just as much a phenomenon of life as man is; it is also a living and speaking fact, and it is less of a 'thing' than all the other things that have been or are being created by man."[2] This statement manifests Gorky's concern for books, for literature, and for culture in general; creativity and talent were sacred to him. It also says much about his approach to writing. In an incisive memoir of Gorky his longtime associate, the poet Vladislav Khodasevich, noted that "this 'great realist' in truth liked only everything that embellished reality; he moved away from it, or did not deal with it, or simply added to it what was missing."[3] Gorky constantly strove to move beyond the often harsh reality that he knew. Inspired, as he says, by books, but also simply by a desire for people to live better than they do, he felt that literature's duty was to instruct, to point the way to a different and finer existence. He ultimately preferred the uplifting dream to the degrading truth.

In his own life he did all he could to further the cause of literature. His rapid emergence as a leader within the *Sreda* group of writers, his intensive work as both editor and publisher, his willingness to encourage both his peers and younger writers, and his tireless efforts to aid his fellow writers after the revolution all speak of a person for whom literature was a noble calling, of no less urgency than the political issues to which he was also committed. To be sure, in the last years of his life Gorky often served as a voice for a regime already on the path toward the purges, in which perished several writers

110

whom Gorky had once helped. Nevertheless, close study of the period indicates that Gorky, who during his years abroad had been skeptical of the government's intentions, worked consistently if not always successfully to protect the literary world from the worst of the political pressures directed against it.[4]

If Gorky's political statements, whatever his intentions, are dubious, there is no doubt that he was a towering literary figure for nearly four decades. His massive output, his extensive publishing activities, and his wide circle of acquaintances make him a writer to be dealt with at length in any history of the period. Still, opinions vary as to the quality of his writing. In the Soviet Union today he is simply regarded as a classic. Articles and books on him often resemble panegyrics. For example, the entry in the *Concise Literary Encyclopedia,* which begins by calling him the "founder of socialist realist literature and the father of Soviet literature," scarcely says a negative word about him, except for a comment on his "Untimely Thoughts,"[5] the sometime anti-Bolshevik column that appeared in the newspaper *Novaya zhizn'* (New Life) in 1917–18. But Gorky was not always accorded such iconic treatment. In the previous *Literary Encyclopedia,* I. M. Bespalov (who died in the purges) wrote a much more balanced critique. His article appeared in 1929, when Gorky was still dividing his time between Russia and Italy and had not yet become untouchable. After summarizing the main distinguishing features of Gorky's writing, Bespalov offers a less than enthusiastic general evaluation: "Gorky's works are constructed through the mechanical accumulation of situations, events, nature descriptions, everyday life, the external appearances of characters, etc." He notes that some elements "are introduced not because they are necessary for the main plot or for the characterization of images, but because of their independent importance."[6] The tone of the piece is hardly negative, but it does take a more realistic view of the writer and his accomplishments than many more recent assessments.

In the West Gorky's reputation has diminished. Widely respected during his lifetime, he has been treated coolly, when at all, by more recent critics. As we have seen, the one work still universally associated with his name is *The Lower Depths,* but few Western readers know a broad range of his writings. While several other plays of his have been revived on occasion, among his prose works only a handful of stories and his memoirs are familiar to any but specialists.

This study has suggested that many of Gorky's lesser-known works would repay close study. In particular, his sprawling novel *The Life of Matvei Kozhemiakin* marks a turning point in his career. Its subject matter foreshadows Gorky's novels of the 1920s, but, more important, its manner offers the first hints at the qualities that make his autobiographical writings so successful. Also of interest are his plays of the 1910s, few of which have received many performances abroad. His final plays of that period—*The Zykovs, The Counterfeit Coin, The Old Man*—are especially noteworthy and are totally different from his earlier dramatic works, with which audiences are much more likely to be familiar. While Gorky's short pieces have always had a good reputation, only a relatively narrow selection of his stories is readily available in English. Many of his short autobiographical and semiautobiographical works are hardly inferior to the tales usually anthologized. This is not to suggest that everything Gorky produced is of equal value, for he wrote prolifically and at times unevenly. Nonetheless, he left a large body of work that awaits rediscovery.

This study has also urged that an appreciation of Gorky's writing depends at least in part on an understanding of his literary methods. Throughout his career he broke the accepted rules for creating a well-made story and instead, as Bespalov noted, incorporated numerous disparate elements into his writing. In his mature work he favored a fragmentary presentation that ignored the conventions of plot and structure. At its worst the technique produced some forgettable tales, but at its best it led to masterful portrayals, as in his memoirs of Tolstoy.

Too often readers have approached Gorky in expectation of a simple narrative and a neatly constructed tale, whereas Gorky preferred a convoluted and multifaceted approach. In both his manner of writing and the breadth of his achievement he turns out to be a more complex and more accomplished author than his reputation in the West would indicate.

Notes and References

Chapter One

1. Dates prior to 1918 are given in the "old style," that is according to the Julian calendar, which was twelve days behind the Gregorian in the nineteenth century and thirteen days behind in the twentieth.

2. In the Soviet Union Gorky is sometimes referred to as "M. Gorky" and sometimes as "A. M. Gorky"; in the latter case his real initials are combined with his pseudonym. It is not unusual to find references both to M. Gorky and to A. M. Gorky within the same book. Some authorities have recommended, though with limited success, that M. Gorky be used when the topic is primarily his literary work and that A. M. Gorky be preferred for instances when the focus is on his social and political activities or on his entire career. See K. D. Muratova, ed., *Istoriia russkoi literatury kontsa XIX-nachala XX veka: Bibliograficheskii ukazatel'* [History of Russian Literature at the End of the Nineteenth and the Beginning of the Twentieth Centuries: Bibliography] (Moscow and Leningrad: AN SSSR 1963), 187.

3. On Vasily Kashirin's background, see N. A. Zaburdaev, *V sem'e Kashirinykh* [The Kashirin Family] (Gorky: Volgo-viatskoe knizhnoe izdatel'stvo, 1976), 14–27 and 38–56.

4. The decline of generations appears in several of Gorky's novels, including *Foma Gordeev* (see Chap. 3) and *The Artamonov Business* (Chap. 6). For references to discussions of this theme, see nn. 3 and 4 to Chap. 3.

5. On Gorky's social origins, see Alexander Kaun, *Maxim Gorky and His Russia* (New York: J. Cape and H. Smith, 1931), 317–18.

6. Information about Maximov is given in Zaburdaev, *V sem'e Kashirinykh,* 153–60.

7. For a detailed discussion of Gorky's early reading, see Il'ia Gruzdev, *Gor'kii i ego vremia, 1868–1896* [Gorky and His Time, 1868–1896], 3d ed., enl. (Mocow: GIKhL, 1962), 37–57.

8. The poet Vladislav Khodasevich comments on this quality in an excellent memoir of Gorky in his *Nekropol': Vospominaniia* [Necropolis: Memoirs] (1939; reprint ed., Paris: YMCA-Press 1976), 254.

9. V. A. Desnitskii, "M. Gor'kii Nizhegorodskikh let" [Gorky in Nizhny Novgorod] in *A. M. Gor'kii: Ocherki zhizni i tvorchestva* [M. Gorky: Sketches of His Life and Work] (Moscow: GIKhL 1959), 47, mentions that Gorky during his time in Nizhny Novgorod had revolutionary sym-

pathies but had not accepted (or perhaps even fully considered) the theoretical positions of the Social Democratic party.

10. There are still questions about Gorky's precise activities even during 1891, the most fully documented of those years. R G. Beislekhem and R. M. Vul', "Zametki o stranstviiakh Gor'kogo" [Notes on Gorky's Wanderings], in *Gor'kovskie chteniia, vol. 10, K stoletiiu so dnia rozhdeniia pisatelia* [Readings on Gorky; vol. 10, For the Centennial of the Writer's Birth] (Moscow: Nauka, 1968), 365. The fullest account of Gorky's wanderings is to be found in Gruzdev *Gor'kii,* while for those who do not know Russian Kaun's *Maxim Gorky* still offers much valuable information.

11. The stages in Gorky's wanderings from his arrival at the Caspian Sea in 1888 until his return to Nizhny Novgorod in the spring of the following year are given in *Letopis' zhizni i tvorchestva A. M. Gor'kogo* [A Chronology of A. M. Gorky's Life and Work], ed. Akademiia Nauk SSSR, 4 vols. (Moscow: AN SSSR, *1958–60*), vol. 1, *1868–1907, 59–65.* As the Russian indicates, all four volumes in this publication are "chronicles," with much factual information but little in the way of selection, ordering, or interpretation. Still, they are particularly valuable for gaining a quick overview of the periods when Gorky was on his travels.

12. Gorky described this encounter in his essay "Korolenko and His Times." Korolenko acknowledged the visit in a not particularly enthusiastic assessment of the poem Gorky had shown him: A. M. Gor'kii and V. G. Korolenko, *Perepiska, stat'i, vyskazyvaniia* [Correspondence, Letters, Comments] (Moscow: GIKhL, 1957), 25.

13. On his relationship with Kaminskaya, see Filia Holtzman, *The Young Maxim Gorky, 1868–1902* (New York: Columbia University Press, 1948), 13–24. Gorky himself described their relationship some thirty years later in the story "About a First Love" ("O pervoi liubvi," 1923).

14. Gorky's contributions to the Kazan newspaper *Volzhskii vestnik* [Volga Herald] are described by E. G. Bushkanets, "A. M. Gor'kii i *Volzhskii vestnik*" [Gorky and the *Volga Herald*], *Gor'kovskie chteniia, vol. 4, 1949–1952* [Readings on Gorky, Vol. 4, 1949–52] (Moscow: AN SSSR, 1954), 406–13. When Gorky began to publish there it had a liberal reputation, but it soon began to move to the right and Gorky's connection with it ceased.

15. On Gorky's editorship at this paper, see R. M. Vul', "Pervoe redaktorstvo A. M. Gor'kogo [Gorky's First Editorship]," in *Gor'kovskie chteniia,* 10:224–46.

16. F. P. Khitrovskii, "Gor'kii v redaktsii *Nizhegorodskogo listka* (Iz vospominanii) [Gorky at the Editorial Offices of the *Nizhny Novgorod News* (Memoirs)]," in *M. Gor'kii v vospominaniiakh sovremennikov* [Gorky in the Memoirs of his Contemporaries], ed. A. S. Miasnikov and A. I. Lektorskii (Moscow: GIKhL, 1955), 109.

17. Kaun, *Maxim Gorky,* 260.

18. Much of this paragraph is based on the informative article by Mary Louise Loe, "Maksim Gor'kii and the *Sreda* Circle: 1899–1905," *Slavic Review* 44 no. 1 (1985):49–66.

19. Eventually some forty of these anthologies were published; they also included translations of works by some of the leading foreign authors. For a thorough treatment of the entire *Znanie* enterprise, see O. D. Golubeva, *Gor'kii—izdatel'* [Gorky as Publisher] (Moscow: Kniga 1968), 5–57.

20. *Arkhiv A. M. Gor'kogo* [The Gorky Archive] vol. 4, (Moscow: GIKhL, 1954), 246; letter of 17 April 1908.

21. Ibid., 121; letter written between 17 and 19 February 1903.

22. *Literaturnoe nasledstvo* [Literary Heritage] 72 (1965):121–22; letters of 23 December 1901 and of 26–28 December 1901.

23. For an extensive description of Gorky's relationship with his fellow *Znanie* writers, see A. A. Volkov, *M. Gor'kii i literaturnoe dvizhenie kontsa XIX i nachala XX vekov* [Gorky and the Literary Movement of the Late Nineteenth and Early Twentieth Centuries] (Moscow: Sovetskii pisatel', 1954), 110–80.

24. Skitalets himself described their first contacts in a memoir devoted to Gorky; see his *Izbrannye proizvedeniia* [Selected Works] (Moscow: Khudozhestvennaia literatura, 1955), especially 579–80 and 591–95.

25. The history of Gorky's literary relationship with Skitalets is given in M. G. Petrova, "V shkole Gor'kogo (O tvorchestve Skital'tsa)" [The Art of Skitalets], in *Gor'kovskie chteniia, vol. 9, 1964–1965* [Readings on Gorky, vol. 9, 1964–65] (Moscow: Nauka, 1966), 162–225. She describes Gorky's disillusionment with Skitalets on 217–25.

26. A. A. Ninov, *M. Gor'kii i Iv. Bunin: Istoriia otnosheniiproblemy tvorchestva* [Gorky and Bunin: Their Relations and Questions of Their Art] (Leningrad: Sovetskii pisatel', 1973), 204, 220, et passim.

27. Ibid., 402–12, 431.

28. Nina Berberova, *The Italics Are Mine* (New York: Harcourt, Brace, and World, 1969), 182–83. In Berberova's account, Gorky was so taken by a collection of Bunin's stories that he abandoned his scheduled work for the day to read it; for some time afterwards he found it impossible to read Soviet "best-sellers" or the unsolicited manuscripts that he usually willingly reviewed.

29. Lists of Gorky's works translated into foreign languages are given at the end of the chronicle for each year in the *Letopis'*. In 1901 alone *Foma Gordeev* came out in English, French, German, Hungarian, Czech, Serbian, and Croatian. Other works to appear in English that year included "Creatures That Once Were Men," "Konovalov," "Malva," and "The Orlovs." (*Letopis'*, 1:362–63.)

30. On this incident, see V. I. Kachalov, "Iz vospominanii [From My Memoirs]," in *M. Gor'kii v vospominaniiakh sovremennikov*, 210–11.

31. A summary of Andreeva's career and of her relationship with Gorky can be found in A. P. Grigor'eva and S. V. Shchirina, "Osnovnye etapy zhizni i deiatel'nosti M. F. Andreevoi" [Basic Stages of M. F. Andreeva's Life and Work], in Mariia Fedorovna Andreeva, *Perepiska, vospominaniia, stat'i, dokumenty, vospominaniia o M. F. Andreevoi* [Correspondence, Memoirs, Articles, Documents, Memoirs about M. F. Andreeva], 3d ed., rev. and enl. (Moscow: Iskusstvo, 1968), 577–658.

32. Much of this paragraph is based on M. R. Werner, "L'Affaire Gorky," *New Yorker,* 30 April 1949, 62–73.

33. On the visits by Andreev and Bunin, see L. V. Bykovtseva, *Gor'kii v Italii* [Gorky in Italy] (Moscow: Sovetskii pisatel', 1975), 90–97. On 68–76 she discusses the whole "Russian colony" that came into existence on Capri during Gorky's stay there.

34. On the final years of *Znanie,* see Golubeva, *Gor'kii—izdatel',* 44–55.

35. A good summary of the "God-building" movement can be found in Christopher Read, *Religion, Revolution and the Russian Intelligentsia 1900–1912: The Vekhi Debate and Its Intellectual Background* (London: Macmillan, 1979), 77–94.

36. George L. Kline, *Religious and Anti-Religious Thought in Russia* (Chicago: University of Chicago Press, 1968), 112.

37. The attempt to establish a school for workers on Capri is discussed in Bertram D. Wolfe, *The Bridge and the Abyss: The Troubled Friendship of Maxim Gorky and V. I. Lenin* (New York: Praegar 1967), 47–49.

38. This supposed decline followed by Gorky's revival as an artist was noted by the contemporary critic V. L. L'vov-Rogachevskii: see his "Maksim Gor'kii," *Russkaia literatura XX veka (1890–1910)* [Twentieth-century Russian Literature (1890–1910)], ed. S. A. Vengerov, 3 vols. (Moscow: Mir, 1914–16), 1:217–25.

39. In a letter to Ekaterina Pavlovna Peshkova, his former wife, Gorky states that his nerves and mood are both in poor shape and says that "things are going badly for Russia." *Arkhiv A. M. Gor'kogo,* vol. 9 (Moscow: GIKhL, 1966), 204–5. Letter of 2 December 1917.

40. The history of Gorky's activities during the period 1918–21 is based upon Barry P. Scherr, "Notes on Literary Life in Petrograd, 1918–1922: A Tale of Three Houses," *Slavic Review* 36, no. 2 (1977):256–67.

41. Golubeva, *Gor'kii-izdatel',* 98–108.

42. A. D. Zaidman, "Literaturnye studii 'Vsemirnoi literatury' i 'Doma iskusstv' (1919–1921 gody)" [Literary Workshops of "World Literature" and "House of the Arts" in the years 1919–21], *Russkaia literatura* [Russian Literature] 16, no. 1 (1973):142–45.

43. Kornei Chukovskii, *Sovremenniki* [Contemporaries], vol. 2 of *Sobranie sochinenii v shesti tomakh* [Collected works in Six Volumes] (Moscow: Khudozhestvennaia literatura, 1965–69), 486.

44. P. P. Shirmakov, "K istorii literaturno-khudozhestvennykh ob"edinenii pervykh let Sovetskoi vlasti: Soiuz deiatelei khudozhestvennoi literatury (1918–1919 gody)" [On the History of Literary and Artistic Circles during the First Years of Soviet Power: The Union of Belletrists (1918–1919)], *Voprosy sovetskoi literatury* [Problems of Soviet Literature] 7 (1958):461–62. See also 463–71 of this article for further details regarding plans for publishing works under the aegis of the Union of Belletrists.

45. Many of those who lived at the House of the Arts wrote about it. In addition to Chukovsky's memoirs (see n. 43 above) good descriptions of the facilities at the house can be found in Vs. A. Rozhdestvenskii, *Stranitsy zhizni: Iz literaturnykh vospominanii* [Life's Pages: From My Literary Memoirs], 2d ed., enl. (Moscow: Sovremennik, 1974), 263–66, and by V. F. Khodasevich, *Literaturnye stat'i i vospominaniia* [Literary Articles and Memoirs] (New York: Chekhov Publishing House, 1954), 401–5. Articles devoted specifically to life in the House of the Arts include Anna El'kan, "Dom iskusstv [The House of the Arts]," *Mosty* [Bridges], no. 5 (1960), 289–98; and Vladimir Milashevskii, "V dome na Moike: Iz zapisok khudozhnika [At the House on the Moika: From an Artist's Notes]," *Zvezda* [Star] 47, no. 12 (1970): 187–201. Most unusual of all is the roman à clef by Ol'ga Forsh, *Sumasshedshii korabl'* [Lunatic Ship] (Leningrad: Izd. Pisatelei v Leningrade, 1931), in which many of the house's residents appear under fictitious names.

46. On the activities at the House of the Arts, see Zaidman, "Literaturnye studii," 146 and Chukovskii, *Sovremenniki,* 504–5.

47. For a description of Gorky's role in establishing the Scholars' House, see A. A. Borisov, "A. M. Gor'kii—organizator pervogo Doma uchenykh" [Gorky as Organizer of the First Scholars' House] in *Gor'kovskie chteniia,* 10:322–32.

48. Konstantin Fedin, *Gor'kii sredi nas: Kartiny literaturnoi zhizni* [Gorky among Us: Pictures of Literary Life] (Moscow: Molodaia gvardiia, 1967), 46–47. For an overview of Gorky's efforts on behalf of Russian writers from the revolution into the 1930s, see Irwin Weil, *Gorky: His Literary Development and Influence on Soviet Intellectual Life* (New York: Random House, 1966), chap. 4, 104–32.

49. Gorky, letter written in spring 1921, *Literaturnoe nasledstvo* 70 (1963):170.

50. Ibid., Gorky, letter of 10 October 1922, 172–73.

51. V. B. Shklovskii, *Sentimental'noe puteshestvie; Vospominaniia 1917– 1922* [Sentimental Journey: Memoirs 1917–1922] (Moscow and Berlin: Gelikon, 1923), 265–67 and 381. On the relationship of Shklovsky to both Gorky and the Serapions, see Richard Sheldon, "Šklovskij, Gor'kij and the Serapion Brothers," *Slavic and East European Journal* 12, no 1 (1968):1–13.

52. On Gorky's conflicts with Zinovev, see V. F. Khodasevich, *Iz-*

brannaia proza v dvukh tomakh [Selected Prose in Two Volumes] (New York: Serebrianyi vek, 1982), *Belyi koridor: Vospominaniia* [The White Corridor: Memoirs], 227–31.

53. The information regarding Moura Budberg is based on the extensive biography by Nina Berberova, *Zheleznaia zhenshchina: Rasskaz o zhizni M. I. Zakrevskoi-Benkendorf-Budberg, o nei samoi i ee druz'iakh* [Iron Woman: The Story of the Life of M. I. Zakrevskaya-Benkendorf-Budberg, On Her and on Her Friends], 2d ed., rev. (New York: Russica, 1982).

54. On the history of the *Chronicle,* see L. Fleishman, R. Hughes, and O. Raevskaia-Hughes, *Russkii Berlin, 1921–1923: Po materialam Arkhiva B. I. Nikolaevskogo v Guverovskom Institute* [Russian Berlin 1921–23: Materials from the Nikolaevsky Archive at the Hoover Institution] (Paris: YMCA, 1983), 350–58.

55. Khodasevich has described the financial crisis caused by the inability to sell *Beseda* within the Soviet Union. See his *Izbrannaia proza* [Selected Prose], 1:236–38.

56. To many contemporaries it appeared that Gorky would continue to divide his time between Italy and the Soviet Union indefinitely; see Kaun, *Maxim Gorky,* 546. Kaun, though, correctly predicted that Gorky' would find it difficult to write the concluding volume of *The Life of Klim Samgin.*

57. Bykovtseva, *Gor'kii v Italii,* 285–92.

58. Khodasevich, *Izbrannaia proza,* 1:244–45.

59. Kaun, *Maxim Gorky,* 521–23.

60. *Arkhiv A. M. Gor'kogo,* vol. 11 (Moscow: Nauka, 1966), 183; letter to Il'ia Gruzdev of 17 November 1928.

61. Nina Gourfinkel, *Gorky,* trans. Ann Feshbach (New York: Grove Press, 1960), 87–88.

62. Fleishman, Hughes, and Raevskaia-Hughes, *Russkii Berlin,* 341–50, describe Gorky's efforts to prevent the execution of the Socialist Revolutionaries.

63. Letter of 8 November 1923, published in *Harvard Slavic Studies* 1 (1953): 306–7.

64. Nina Berberova remarks that after Lenin's death Gorky began to revise his views on the revolution and on the early years of Bolshevik rule. *Zheleznaia zhenshchina,* 216 (cf. 200).

65. See, for example, his letter of 8 November 1921 to Ekaterina Pavlovna, in which he tries to reassure her about her son's rumored drinking: *Arkhiv A. M. Gor'kogo,* 9:213–14. Earlier in a letter of 13 September 1916 (189), he urges his son to pay more attention to his studies.

66. Khodasevich, *Izbrannaia proza,* 1:246–47.

67. Ibid., 254.

68. Bykovtseva, *Gor'kii v Italii,* 5.

69. See Gorky's introductory chapter "Pravda sotsializma [The Truth

of Socialism]," In *Belomorsko-Baltiiskii kanal imeni Stalina: Istoriia stro-itel'stva* [The Stalin Canal from the White to the Baltic Sea: History of Its Construction], ed. M. Gor'kii, L. Averbakh, and S. Firin (Moscow: Istoriia fabrik i zavodov, 1934), esp. 12, 14–15, 17–19.

70. For instance, in the course of his frequent letters to A. B. Khalatov, who headed Gosizdat, the State Publishing House, from 1927 through 1932, Gorky offered blunt advice about what should (and should not) be published. In one letter he both complains about the selection of foreign writers and admonishes Khalatov for allowing abridgments of classical literature in the inexpensive editions that Gosizdat was putting out. *Arkhiv A. M. Gor'kogo*, vol. 10, bk. 1 (Moscow: Nauka, 1964) 177–78. Gorky's involvement with the Academia Publishing House is described in L. N. Iokar, "Gor'kii v izdatel'stve 'Academia' [Gorky at the Academia Publishing House]", in *Gor'kovskie chteniia* 10:289–306.

71. Khodasevich, *Izbrannaia proza*, 1:263–71.

72. Alexander Orlov, *The Secret History of Stalin's Crimes* (New York: Random House, 1953), 261–76. On 261–62 he specifically asserts that both Gorky and his son died of natural causes.

73. Berberova, *Zheleznaia zhenshchina*, 295–305. She does note that two accounts indicating Gorky was murdered seem more convincing than the others, but also remarks that they are indirect. Berberova herself feels that Gorky's son definitely died a violent death, adding that doubts about Gorky's own death still exist (299).

Chapter Two

1. M. Gor'kii, *Polnoe sobranie sochinenii: Khudozhestvennye proizvedeniia v dvadtsati piati tomakh* [Complete Works: Artistic Works in Twenty-Five Volumes] (Moscow: Nauka, 1968–76), 1:6–8. Further references to this edition are included in the text by volume number and page.

2. Vengerov, ed. *Russkaia literatura XX veka*, 1:195.

3. On the use of folklore elements in this work, see M. P. Shustov, "K probleme skazochnosti stilia M. Gor'kogo ('Makar Chudra') [On the Problem of Gorky's Use of *Skaz* Style ('Makar Chudra')]", *M. Gor'kii i voprosy literaturnykh zhanrov* [Gorky and Problems of Literary Genres], ed. I. K. Kuz'michev (Gorky: Gor'kovskii gosudarstvennyi universitet, 1978), 115–22. For a more general study of folklore influences on Gorky's early work, see N. F. Matveichuk, *V tvorcheskoi masterskoi M. Gor'kogo* [In Gorky's Artistic Workshop] (Lvov: L'vovskii gosudarstvennyi universitet, 1982), 12–42.

4. On his arrival in the United States in 1906 he remarked that "Old Izergil"—"the story that I consider to be my best"—had not yet been translated into English (though, as it happens, a translation had just been published in England the previous year). S. S. Elizarov et al., eds.,

M. Gor'kii v epokhu revoliutsii 1905–1907 godov: Materialy, vospominaniia.
issledovaniia [Gorky during the Revolutionary Period of 1905–1907: Materials, Memoirs, Investigations] (Moscow: AN SSSR, 1957), 390.
    5. B.V. Mikhailovskii and E. B. Tager, *Tvorchestvo M. Gor'kogo*
[Gorky's Art], 3d ed., rev. (Moscow: Prosveshchenie, 1969), 11.
    6. For a detailed analysis of this fable, see F. M. Borras, *Maxim Gorky the Writer: An Interpretation* (Oxford: Clarendon Press, 1967), 34–36.
    7. On the sources for this work in both literature and folklore, see S. D. Balukhatyi, "Pesnia o Sokole [Song of the Falcon]," in *M. Gor'kii: Materialy i issledovaniia* [Gorky: Materials and Investigations], 4 vols. (Leningrad: AN SSSR, 1934–51), 3(1941): 161–273. For treatment of still another possible source, see V. E. Gusev, "K voprosu o fol'klornom istochnike 'Pesni o Sokole' A. M. Gor'kogo [On the Question of a Folklore Source for Gorky's 'Song of the Falcon']," *Russkii fol'klor* [Russian Folklore] 4 (1959):268–74.
    8. Betty Y. Forman, "Nietzsche and Gorky in the 1890s: The Case for an Early Influence," in *Western Philosophical Systems in Russian Literature: A Collection of Critical Studies,* ed. Anthony M. Mlikotin (Los Angeles: University of Southern California Press, 1979), 158–60.
    9. Ibid., 156 and 161. Soviet critics have strongly denied any positive interest on Gorky's part in Nietzsche's ideas. See in particular the extensive discussion by N. E. Krutikova, *V nachale veka: Gor'kii i simvolisty* [A Century Begins: Gorky and the Symbolists] (Kiev: Naukova dumka 1978), 120–201. But even she has some difficulty in dealing with Gorky's views during the 1890's. Not only the so-called "bourgeois" critics, but even Marxists such as Lunacharsky discerned Nietzschean elements in the early Gorky (152–54). And Gorky himself expressed some admiration for Nietzsche in a letter of 1897 (180–83).
    10. On possible inspirations for Gorky's use of the stormy petrel as a symbol, see N. S. Travushkin. "Burevestnik do i posle Gor'kogo (simvol, metafora, slovo-signal) [The Stormy Petrel before and after Gorky (Symbol, Metaphor, Signal Word)]," *Russkaia literatura {Russian Literature}* 26, no. 4 (1983): 158–64.
    11. Lenin himself quoted the last line of the story to conclude a 1906 article, "Before the Storm," in *Polnoe sobranie sochinenii* [Complete Works], 5th ed., vol. 13 (Moscow: Izd. Politicheskoi literatury, 1960), 337–38.
    12. For a concise description of the *bosiak*'s main characteristics, see Loe, "Maksim Gor'kii and the *Sreda* Cicle," 50–51.
    13. A. P. Chekhov, *Polnoe sobranie sochinenii i pisem v tridtsati tomakh: Pis'ma v dvenadtsati tomakh* [Complete Works and Letters in Thirty Volumes: Letters in Twelve Volumes] (Moscow: Nauka, 1974–83), 7:352.

Further references to this edition will consist of *Pis'ma* [Letters] followed by volume and page number.

14. The twenty-five volumes of Gorky's literary writings in his complete collected works (see n. 1 to this chapter) are supplemented by ten volumes of variants (referred to subsequently as *Varianty*). This passage is in *Varianty*, 1:138; cf. the final version in 2:24.

15. For a detailed analysis of Gorky's extensive revisions of "Chelkash," see N. Brodskii, "Rabota M. Gor'kogo nad 'Chelkashem' [Gorky's Work on 'Chelkash'],'' *Literaturnyi kritik* [Literary Critic] 7, no. 2 (1939): 184–210.

16. *Arkhiv A. M. Gor'kogo,* 11(1966):66.

17. M. Gor'kii, *Sobranie sochinenii v tridtsati tomakh* [Collected Works in Thirty Volumes] (Moscow: GIKhL 1949–56), 25:322. Subsequent references to this edition are by *G-30,* followed by volume and page number.

18. This point has been made by many critics; see for instance Ivanov-Razumnik, *Istoriia russkoi obshchestvennoi mysli* [History of Russian Social Thought] 2 vols. 4th ed., (Saint Petersburg: M. M. Stasiulevich, 1914), 2:403–4.

19. As it turns out, the newspaper article Gorky read apparently referred to a different Konovalov; the person Gorky had known died a few years after the story was written (3:542–43).

20. This presence of a vague but destructive dissatisfaction with life, the sense of an unbridgeable gulf between the ideal and the actual, caused critics to see a certain similarity between Gorky and Lermontov. S. V. Zaika, "Tvorchestvo A. M. Gor'kogo i problema literaturnoi preemstvennosti (90–e—nachalo 900–x godov) [Gorky's Art and the Problem of Literary Influences from the 1890s to the 1900s],'' *Russkaia literatura* [Russian Literature] 25, no. 1 (1982):27–28.

21. On "critical realism" and "naturalism" in Russian literature of this period, see B. V. Mikhailovskii, *Russkaia literatura XX veka* [Twentieth-Century Russian Literature] (Moscow: Uchpedgiz, 1939), 22–47.

22. Chekhov tended to refer to both stories together, though in his letters he singles out "In the Steppe" for special praise. See his 1899 letters to the publisher A. S. Suvorin *(Pis'ma,* 8:52) and the dramatist P. P. Gnedich *(Pis'ma,* 8:70).

23. Mikhailovskii and Tager, *Tvorchestvo M. Gor'kogo,* 30. They include some of Gorky's early stories in this group, but Gorky's greatest successes with this technique occur in the late 1890's.

24. V. V. Vorovskii, *Literaturno-kriticheskie stat'i* [Literary Critical Articles] (Moscow: GIKhL, 1956), 258.

25. L. Michael O'Toole, *Structure, Style and Interpretation in the Russian Short Story* (New Haven: Yale University Press, 1982), 130.

26. George Gutsche, "The Role of the 'One' in Gor'kij's 'Twenty-

Six and One'," in *Studies in Honor of Xenia Gasiorowska,* ed. Lauren G. Leighton (Columbus: Slavica, 1983), 49–50.

27. Helen Muchnic, *From Gorky to Pasternak: Six Writers in Soviet Russia* (New York: Random House, 1961), 72.

28. On the role of the baker, see O'Toole, *Structure, Style and Interpretation,* 133–34.

29. This theme is emphasized by E. I. Babaian, *Rannii Gor'kii: U ideinikh istokov tvorchestva* [The Early Gorky: Ideological Sources of His Art] (Moscow: Khudozhestvennaia literatura, 1973), 167–68.

Chapter Three

1. This opinion is offered by, among others, Helen Muchnic, in *From Gorky to Pasternak,* 85.

2. B. V. Mikhailovskii, "Roman *Foma Gordeev* [The Novel *Foma Gordeev*]," *Gor'kovskie chteniia,* 6(1961):134.

3. The family theme in this and other Russian works is discussed by Mikhailovskii, "Roman *Foma Gordeev,*" 140–47.

4. On these last two works see Barry Scherr, "Time, Space, and Causality in the World of Bunin's *Sukhodol,*" *Proceedings: Pacific Northwest Conference on Foreign Languages* 27, pt. 1 (1976):141–45.

5. On the contradictions in Shchurov, see Richard Hare, *Maxim Gorky: Romantic Realist and Conservative Revolutionary* (London, 1962), 62.

6. N. I. Zheltova, "O iazyke povesti M. Gor'kogo *Foma Gordeev* (Tekstologicheskie nabliudeniia) [On the Language of Gorky's Novel *Foma Gordeev*: Textological Observations]," *Voprosy sovetskoi literatury* [Problems of Soviet Literature] 2 (1953):299–308.

7. N. F. Matveichuk, "Poslovitsy i pogovorki v povesti Gor'kogo *Foma Gordeev* [Proverbs and Sayings in Gorky's Novel *Foma Gordeev*]," *Russkii fol'klor* [Russian Folklore] 1 (1956):135–51.

8. On these changes in the novel, see 4:615.

9. Borras, *Maxim Gorky,* 104–5.

10. V. N. Lanina, "Obraz Il'i Luneva (Glava iz monografii o romane M. Gor'kogo *Troe* [The Image of Ilya Lunev (Chapter from a Monograph on Gorky's Novel *The Three of Them*)]," in *Gor'kovskie chteniia, vol. 2, 1947–1948* [Readings on Gorky, vol. 2, 1947–1948], (Moscow: AN SSSR, 1949), 187.

11. On Grachev's poetry, see A. I. Ovcharenko, "Obraz Pavla Gracheva [The Image of Pavel Grachev]," in *Gor'kovskie chteniia, vol. 3, 1949–1950* [Readings on Gorky, vol. 3, 1949–1950] (Moscow: AN SSSR, 1951), 405–14.

12. For a summary of the changes in the novel see S. V. Kastorskii, *Povest' M. Gor'kogo* Mat': *Ee obshchestvenno-politicheskoe i literaturnoe znachenie* [Gorky's Novel *Mother:* Its Social, Political, and Literary Significance]

(Leningrad: Uchpedgiz, 1954), 60–69; a more detailed examination of the way in which specific episodes and characters were reworked can be found on 70–104. An earlier version of this section, along with a full analysis of the differences between the London and New York editions, appeared as "Iz istorii sozdaniia povesti *Mat'* (O pervonachal'nom tekste povesti) [From the History of the Creation of *Mother* (On the Novel's Original Text)]," in *M. Gor'kii: Materialy i issledovaniia,* 3 (1941):288–360. A Soviet translation into English of the later edition is currently in print along with the Isidore Schneider translation of the original version.

13. For an extensive commentary on the real-life sources for *Mother,* see I. V. Nikitina, *Po sledam geroev Gor'kogo (Nizhegorodskii kommentarii k proizvedeniiam pisatelia)* [On the Trail of Gorky's Heroes (A Nizhny Novgorod Commentary on the Writer's Works)] (Gorky: Volgo–viatskoe knizhnoe izdatel'stvo, 1951), 17–63.

14. Rufus W. Mathewson, Jr., *The Positive Hero in Russian Literature,* 2d ed. (Stanford: Stanford University Press, 1975), 167.

15. B. I. Bursov, *Roman M. Gor'kogo* Mat' [Gorky's Novel *Mother*] (Moscow and Leningrad: Khudozhestvennaia literatura, 1962), 110–17. On the importance of the novel as providing a cornerstone for what came to be known as socialist realism, see Bursov's *Mat' M. Gor'kogo i voprosy sotsialisticheskogo realizma* [Gorky's *Mother* and Problems of Socialist Realism] (Moscow and Leningrad: Khudozhestvennaia literatura, 1951).

16. Richard Freeborn, *The Russian Revolutionary Novel: Turgenev to Pasternak* Cambridge: Cambridge University Press, 1982), 52. On the mythological qualities of the novel, see also Mette Bryld, "M. Gor'kijs *Mat':* Eine mythische Wanderung [Gorky's *Mother:* A Mythical Journey]," *Scando-Slavica* 28 (1982):27–49.

17. L. A. Kolobaeva, "Avtor i geroi v romane M. Gor'kogo *Mat'* [Author and Hero in Gorky's Novel *Mother*]," *Aktual'nye problemy sotsialisticheskogo realizma* [Current Problems of Socialist Realism], ed. I. F. Volkov et al. (Moscow: Izd. Moskovskogo universiteta, 1981), 189.

18. Freeborn, *Russian Revolutionary Novel,* 50–51.

19. Gorky mentioned a three-part novel to be called *Pavel Vlasov* in a letter to I. P. Ladyzhnikov dated 11 February 1907. *Archiv A. M. Gor'kogo,* 7 (1959):156.

20 A. A. Volkov, *Put' khudozhnika: M. Gor'kii do Oktiabria* [The Artist's Way: Gorky before the October Revolution] (Moscow: Khudozhestvennaia literatura, 1969), 213.

21. In an article that deals predominantly with the revolutionary aspects of *A Summer,* S. V. Kastorskii denied that the novel bore any traces of the ideas Gorky had presented in *A Confession: Stat'i o Gor'kom* [Articles on Gorky], (Leningrad: Sovetskii pisatel', 1953), 445–47. More recent critics have seen some influences, e. g., Volkov, *Put' khudozhnika* [The Artist's Way], 208, 212.

22. For a detailed survey of contemporary critical opinion, see 9:538–60.

23. On this episode, see D. M. Stepaniuk, *"Ispoved'* M. Gor'kogo i tsarskaia tsenzura [Gorky's *Confession* and the Tsarist Censorship]," *Voprosy russkoi literatury* [Problems of Russian Literature] 14, no. 2 (1970):78–80.

24. As does Dan Levin in *Stormy Petrel: The Life and Work of Maxim Gorky* (New York: Appleton-Croft, 1965), 146.

25. S. V. Kastorskii, "K istorii 'okurovskogo tsikla' Gor'kogo [On the History of Gorky's "Okurov Cycle"]," *Voprosy sovetskoi literatury* [Problems of Soviet Literature] 6 (1957): 10–22. These pages contain information on both the writing of the two works and on the main differences between them.

26. A. I. Ovcharenko, "Povesti M. Gor'kogo ob 'Okurove' [Gorky's Okurov Novels]," *Izvestiia akademii nauk SSSR,* seriia literatury i iazyka [Bulletin of the USSR Academy of Sciences, Literature and Language Series] 20, no. 2 (1961):117.

27. N. Ovsiannikov, "Okurovskii tsikl Gor'kogo [Gorky's Okurov Cycle]," *Voprosy literatury* [Problems of Literature], 25, no. 5 (1981):201–3.

28. On Gorky's treatment of "Oblomovism," see George Lukács, *Studies in European Realism: A Sociological Survey of the Writings of Balzac, Stendhal, Zola, Tolstoy, Gorki and others* (London: Hillway, 1950), 218–20.

Chapter Four

1. See, for instance, Gorky's enthusiastic comments about *Uncle Vanya* in a letter of November 1898, and his praise for *The Seagull* in a letter written the following month. *M. Gor'kii i A. Chekhov: Perepiska, stat'i, vyskazyvaniia* [Gorky and Chekhov: Correspondence, Articles, Comments], ed. S. D. Balukhatyi (Moscow and Leningrad: AN SSSR, 1937), 10–11 and 15.

2. Chekhov, *Pis'ma,* 10:83 (letter of 24 September 1901).

3. *G-30,* 28:291 (letter of 21 or 22 October 1903).

4. For general remarks on both the similarities and differences between the plays of the two writers, see B. V. Mikhailovskii, *Dramaturgiia M. Gor'kogo epokhi pervoi russkoi revoliutsii* [Gorky's Plays Written at the Time of the First Russian Revolution], 2d ed., enl. (Moscow: Iskusstvo, 1955), 260–71. For a broader comparison of the two, see Iu. Iuzovskii *Maksim Gor'kii i ego dramaturgiia* [Maxim Gorky and His Dramaturgy] (Moscow: Iskusstvo, 1959), 275–316.

5. The prominent Russian stage director G. A. Tovstonogov has commented that many productions of Gorky's plays have emphasized their

publicistic aspects over psychological content; in his own production of *The Petty Bourgeois* he attempted to restore the balance. See his *Zerkalo stseny*, vol. 1, *O professii rezhissera* [Mirror of the Stage: On a Director's Profession], (Leningrad: Iskusstvo, 1980), 130.

6. Chekhov, *Pis'ma*, 10:137–38 and 149 (letters of 13 and 23 December 1901).

7. Ibid., 95–96 (letter of 22 October 1901).

8. *Literaturnoe nasledstvo* [Literary Heritage] 72 (1965):475. By 1904 Andreev's feelings about the play had become more negative; in a letter to Gorky he remarked that "your *Lower Depths* is good, but *The Petty Bourgeois* is bad" (Ibid., 218).

9. On Kleshch's position vis-à-vis the other characters, see D. N. Ovsianiko-Kulikovskii, "Sotsial'nye otbrosy *(Na dne* M. Gor'kogo) [Social Outcasts (Gorky's *Lower Depths)*]," in his *Sobranie sochinenii* [Collected Works], vol. 5, 2d ed., rev. (Saint Petersburg: Izd. I.L. Ovsianiko-Kulikovskoi, 1912),176–79.

10. Muchnic. *From Gorky to Pasternak*, 77.

11. See his article "O p'esakh [On Plays]" (1933), in *G-30*, 26:425–26.

12. Iu. Iuzovskii, *Na dne* M. *Gor'kogo: Idei i obrazy* [Gorky's *Lower Depths:* Ideas and Images] (Moscow: Khudozhestvennaia literarura, 1968), 50–51 et passim, points out the importance of the ideas in this allegory for Gorky's play.

13. Ibid., 126–37, where Iuzovskii describes the contrasting effects produced by the interpretations of different actors in the role of Luka.

14. Chekhov, *Pis'ma* 11:12 (letter of 29 July 1902).

15. L. M. Farber, "Kompozitsionnoe svoeobrazie *Na dne* M. Gor'kogo [The Structural Originality of Gorky's *Lower Depths*]," in *Gor'kovskie chteniia 1976: Materialy konferentsii "A. M. Gor'kii i teatr"* [Readings on Gorky 1976: Materials from the Conference on Gorky and the Theater], ed. I. K. Kuz'michev (Gorky: Volgo-viatskoe knizhnoe izdatel'stvo, 1977), 87–90.

16. For instance, S. V. Kastorskii has said that these three plays from a cycle on the intelligentsia: *Dramaturgiia M. Gor'kogo: Nabliudeniia nad ideino-khudozhestvennoi spetsifikoi* [Gorky's Plays: Observations on Their Specific Ideological and Artistic Traits] (Moscow and Leningrad: AN SSSR, 1963), 42.

17. Originally Gorky portrayed Dvoetochie as a matter-of-fact, determined individual from the start; only as he worked on the play did he decide it would be more effective to have him evolve from aimlessness to commitment. See I. P. Kochetova "Rabota M. Gor'kogo nad tekstom p'esy *Dachniki* [Gorky's Work on the Text of *Summerfolk*]," in *Gor'kovskie chteniia, vol. 5, 1953–1957* [Readings on Gorky, vol. 5, 1953–1957], (Moscow: AN SSSR, 1959), 271–79.

18. Harold B. Segel, *Twentieth-Century Russian Drama: From Gorky to the Present* (New York: Columbia University Press, 1979), 15–16.

19. S. D. Balukhatyi, "Rabota M. Gor'kogo nad p'esoi *Deti solntsa* (Materialy i nabliudeniia) [Gorky's Work on the Play *Children of the Sun* (Materials and Observations)]," *M. Gor'kii: Materialy i issledovaniia*, 1(1934):459–62.

20. Nikitina, *Po sledam geroev M. Gor'kogo*, 112–58 (esp. 122–33).

21. A. V. Lunacharskii, *Sobranie sochinenii v vos'mi tomakh* [Collected Works in Eight Volumes], vol. 2, *M. Gor'kii: Sovetskaia literatura: Stat'i, doklady, rechi (1904–1933)* [M. Gorky: Soviet Literature: Articles, Reports, Speeches (1904–1933)] (Moscow: Khudozhestvennaia literatura, 1964), 34.

22. G. V. Plekhanov, "K psikhologii rabochego dvizheniia (Maksim Gor'kii *Vragi*) [On the Psychology of the Workers' Movement (M. Gorky, *Enemies*)]," in his *Iskusstvo i literatura* [Art and Literature], ed. N. F. Bel'chikov (Moscow: GIKhL, 1948), 738–55.

23. John Simon, *Uneasy Stages: A Chronicle of the New York Theater, 1963–1973* (New York: Random House, 1975), 432–33.

24. This division is given by, among others, B. A. Bialik, *M. Gor'kii—dramaturg* [Gorky as Playwright] (Moscow: Sovetskii pisatel', 1962), 215.

25. For a more detailed comparison of this play with *Summerfolk*, see Kastorskii, *Dramaturgiia M. Gor'kogo*, 92–95.

26. Reviews of a 1970 production at the Long Wharf Theatre in New Haven expressed special praise for the figure of Mastakov and what Henry Hewes (*Saturday Review*, 7 February 1970, 24) termed his "comic self-centeredness." See also Harold Clurman, *Nation*, 9 February 1970, 157.

27. *Arkhiv A. M. Gor'kogo*, vol. 7 (Moscow: GIKhL, 1959), 227; letter of 15 August 1913. Gorky was to attack the dramatic versions of Dostoevsky's novels in two articles: "On Karamazovism" and "More on Karamazovism."

28. On this play as a possible reaction to Dostoevsky's works, see Bialik, *M. Gor'kii—dramaturg*, 300–309.

29. Segel, *Twentieth-Century Russian Drama*, 26–27, calls Sofia the play's real hero.

30. V. S. Nechaeva, "Rabota Gor'kogo nad p'esoi *Fal'shivaia moneta* [Gorky's Work on the play *The Counterfeit Coin*]," *Literaturnoe nasledstvo* 74 (1965):58–69.

31. See 13:535–37 of the *Polnoe sobranie sochinenii* [Complete Works] for the full text of Gorky's remarks.

32. This connection was suggested by Iuzovskii, *Maksim Gor'kii i ego dramaturgiia*, 99–101, and developed by Volkov, *Put' khudozhnika*, 310–13.

33. Bialik, M. *Gor'kii—dramaturg*, 310–11.

34. Kastorskii, *Dramaturgiia M. Gor'kogo*, 121. For a broader discussion of Gorky's possible concerns with Dostoevsky's theme of suffering, see Iuzovskii, *Maksim Gor'kii i ego dramaturgiia*, 161–70.

Chapter Five

1. Critics have particularly singled out his memoir of Tolstoy; see, for instance, Borras, *Maxim Gorky*, 158 and Weil, *Gorky*, 86.

2. For a comparison of this work with *Childhood*, see Barry Scherr, "Gor'kij's *Childhood*: The Autobiography as Fiction," *Slavic and East European Journal* 23, no. 3 (1979) 335–38. Much of the following discussion of *Childhood* is based on this article.

3. V. A. Desnitskii, "K voprosu ob avtobiografichnosti povestei M. Gor'kogo *Detstvo* i *V liudiakh* [The Problem of the Autobiographical Nature of Gorky's Works *Childhood* and *In The World*]," in *A. M. Gor'kii*, 376.

4. The report is quoted in 14:567–68.

5. *G-30*, 25:336–39.

6. For instance, Muchnic, *From Gorky to Pasternak*, 49.

7. L. M. Perelygin, "O rabote M. Gor'kogo nad avtobiograficheskoi trilogiei (Stat'ia vtoraia, *Detstvo*) [Gorky's Work on His Autobiographical Trilogy (Article Two, *Childhood*)]," *Russkaia i zarubezhnaia literatura* [Russian and Foreign Literature] [Alma-Ata], no. 1, (1969), 58; cf. Gor'kii, *Varianty*, 4:303.

8. For an account of the dissolute lives led by Gorky's uncles Mikhail and Yakov Kashirin, see Zaburdaev, *V sem'e Kashirinykh*, 74–93.

9. Ibid., 13–14.

10. Desnitskii, "K voprosu," 372.

11. See Susanna Egan, *Patterns of Experience in Autobiography* (Chapel Hill: University of North Carolina Press, 1984), chap. 2, "Childhood: From Innocence to Experience," which includes a brief discussion of Gorky's *Childhood* (96–98).

12. G. M. Atanov, "Avtobiograficheskaia trilogiia M. Gor'kogo (narodno-poeticheskie istoki v izobrazhenii geroev)" [Gorky's Autobiographical Trilogy (Sources from Folk Poetry in the Depiction of Its Heroes)] *Russkaia literatura* 24, no. 1 (1981), 66–69.

13. For comments on the importance of Good Idea for *In the World* see B. V. Mikhailovskii, "Avtobiograficheskaia trilogiia M. Gor'kogo [Gorky's Autobiographical Trilogy]," in *Izbrannye stat'i o literature i iskusstve* [Selected Articles on Literature and Art] (Moscow: Izd. Moskovskogo universiteta, 1969), 310–11, and N. P. Belkina, "Problema polozhitel'nogo geroia v avtobiograficheskoi trilogii Gor'kogo [The Problem of the Positive Hero in Gorky's Autobiographical Trilogy]," in *Gor'kovskie chteniia*, 2:126.

14. Desnitskii, "V liudiakh [In the World]," in his A. M. Gor'kii, 357–66.

15. V. A. Zakharova, "Fol'klor v povestiakh M. Gor'kogo Detstvo i V liudiakh [Folklore in Gorky's Works Childhood and In the World]," Voprosy sovetskoi literatury [Problems of Soviet Literature] 4 (1956):70.

16. On the somewhat mysterious atmosphere in the opening chapters of the trilogy's second section, see Atanov, "Avtobiograficheskaia trilogiia," 69–71.

17. A. F. Tsirulev, "O putiakh analiza nravstvennogo stanovleniia lichnosti (Avtobiograficheskaia trilogiia M. Gor'kogo) [Methods of Analyzing the Moral Development of the Personality (Gorky's Autobiographical Trilogy)]," M. Gor'kii i voprosy poetiki [Gorky and Problems of Poetics], ed. I. K. Kuz'michev (Gorky: Gor'kovskii gosudarstvennyi universitet, 1982), 65–66. See Tsirulev's bibliography of critical works on the trilogy, "Avtobiograficheskaia trilogiia M. Gor'kogo: Kratkaia bibliografiia (1914–1980 gg.)," 82–84.

18. O. I. Foniakova, "Toponimy Kazani v povesti M. Gor'kogo Moi universitety [Kazan Toponyms in Gorky's Work My Universities]," Vestnik Leningradskogo universiteta [Bulletin of Leningrad University] 35, no. 8 (1980):102.

19. For an account of the subsequent career of Mikhail Romas, see I. A. Gruzdev, Gor'kii i ego vremia 1868–1896 [Gorky and His Time 1868–1896], 3d ed., enl. (Moscow: GIKhL, 1962), 618–25. Gruzdev's book contains much background information about the people Gorky met during this period.

20. Thus, in discussing the Autobiography of Benjamin Franklin William C. Spengemann notes that "the highly particularized boy [is] a far more memorable, more completely realized figure than the rather bland and featureless adult he becomes as he sheds his distinctive, alienating traits." The Forms of Autobiography: Episodes in the History of a Literary Genre (New Haven: Yale University Press, 1980), 56.

21. Letter of September 1912 to D. N. Ovsianiko-Kulikovskii in M. Gor'kii: Materialy i issledovaniia, 3 (1941):152.

22. See Gorky's comments about the sketch (ocherk) and story (rasskaz), quoted in 14:583.

23. V. A. Keldysh, "Ideino-khudozhestvennaia problematika sbornika Po Rusi [Problems Posed in the Collection Through Russia]," in Gor'kovskie chteniia, 5 (1959):149–60.

24. Volkov, Put' khudozhnika, 385.

25. V. Ia. Grechnev, Russkii rasskaz kontsa XIX-XX veka (problematika i poetika zhanra [The Russian Short Story of the Late Nineteenth-Twentieth Century (Problems and Poetics of the Genre)] (Leningrad: Nauka, 1979), 195.

26. Weil, Gorky, 90.

27. L. P. Zhak, *Ot zamysla k voploshcheniiu: V tvorcheskoi masterskoi M. Gor'kogo* [From Conception to Implementation: In Gorky's Artistic Workshop], 2d ed. (Moscow: Sovetskii pisatel', 1983), 86–89, discusses other references to Andreev in Gorky's writings. Note that the memoir on Tolstoy as well can be complemented by what Gorky wrote elsewhere.

28. Mikhailovskii and Tager, *Tvorchestvo M. Gor'kogo,* 205.

29. V. B. Shklovskii, *Udachi i porazheniia Maksima Gor'kogo* [Gorky's Successes and Failures] (Tiflis: Zakkniga, 1926), 40–41.

30. Zhak, *Ot zamysla,* 17. She provides an extensive investigation of the background to and the writing of the memoir on 8–76, along with an analysis of the work itself.

31. Shklovskii, *Udachi i porazheniia,* 42.

32. V. S. Barakhov, "Ocherk 'Lev Tolstoi' [The Sketch 'Lev Tolstoy']," in *Gor'kovskie chteniia,* 5:193–94.

Chapter Six

1. Grechnev, *Russkii rasskaz,* 170–71, 189.

2. A. I. Ovcharenko, *M. Gor'kii i literaturnye iskaniia XX stoletiia* [Gorky and Literary Quests of the Twentieth Century], (Moscow: Sovetskii pisatel', 1971), 70–72.

3. Grechnev, *Russkii rasskaz,* 174.

4. M. M. Prishvin, letter of 10 April 1926, *Literaturnoe nasledstvo* 70 (1963):330.

5. *Arkhiv A. M. Gor'kogo,* vol. 8 (Moscow: GIKhL, 1961), 337.

6. Ovcharenko, *M. Gor'kii i literaturnye iskaniia,* 76. Ovcharenko implies that in Karamora the personality that embodies a scoundrel ("podlets") triumphs over that of a hero; in fact, though, Karamora seems constantly torn among his various personae.

7. Grechnev, *Russkii rasskaz,* 182–83.

8. Kastorskii, *Dramaturgiia M. Gor'kogo,* 148–50.

9. For remarks on this play and *The Zykovs,* see Segel, *Twentieth-Century Russian Drama,* 37.

10. On the addition of the scene with Laptev in the second act, see 19:496.

11. Peter Yershov calls the humorous elements in this play an example of "high comedy." See his *Comedy in the Soviet Theater* (New York: Praeger, 1956), 127–29.

12. For a comparison of Bulychov and Dostigaev, see Bialik, *M. Gor'kii–dramaturg,* 464–65.

13. Kastorskii, *Dramaturgiia M. Gor'kogo,* 158.

14. Bialik, *M. Gor'kii–dramaturg,* 478–79.

15. Soviet critics often prefer the more "integral" figure of the later Vassa. See, for instance, I. A. Bocharova, "Dve Vassy [Two Vassas]," in

Gor'kovskie chteniia, vol. 7, 1959–1960 [Readings on Gorky, vol. 7, 1959–1960], (Moscow: AN SSSR, 1962), 181.

16. V. V. Novikova, "Rabota Gor'kogo nad vtoroi redaktsiei p'esy *Vassa Zheleznova* [Gorky's Revision of the Play *Vassa Zheleznova*]," *Literaturnoe nasledstvo* 74 (1965):183.

17. For an extensive analysis of Gorky's work on this novel, see V. A. Maksimova, "Iz tvorcheskoi istorii romana M. Gor'kogo *Delo Artamonovykh* [From the Creative History of Gorky's Novel *The Artamonov Business*]," in *Gor'kovskie chteniia*, 2:144–70.

18. Ovcharenko, M. *Gor'kii i literaturnye iskaniia*, 132.

19. This scene can be found in Gor'kii, *Varianty*, 5:274–81.

20. Konstantin Fedin, letter of 27 March 1926, *Literaturnoe nasledstvo* 70 (1963):509.

21. On the figure of Tikhon Vyalov, see Shklovskii, *Udachi i porazheniia*, 57–64.

22. Gleb Struve, *Russian Literature under Lenin and Stalin, 1917–1953* (Norman: University of Oklahoma Press, 1971), 62. Cf. as well the negative evaluations by Borras, *Maxim Gorky*, 128.

23. A. P. Chapygin, letter of 5 June 1933, *Literaturnoe nasledstvo* 70 (1963):659.

24. Boris Pasternak, letter of 23 November 1927, ibid., 305.

25. *Arkhiv A. M. Gor'kogo*, vol. 10, bk. 2, p. 372; letter of 21 August 1931 to V. Ia. Zazubrin.

26. On the chronological inconsistencies between vols. 3 and 4, see 24:579.

27. A. I. Ovcharenko, *Roman-epopeia M. Gor'kogo* Zhizn' Klima Samgina [Gorky's Epic Novel *The Life of Klim Samgin*], (Moscow: Khudozhestvennaia literatura, 1965), 24.

28. For some of Gorky's notes on the possible endings to this novel, see 24:585–89.

29. N. P. Belkina, "*Zhizn' Klima Samgina* (Glavnye obrazy romana) [*The Life of Klim Samgin* (Major Images in the Novel)]," in *Gor'kovskie chteniia, vol. 3, 1949–1950* [Readings on Gorky, vol. 3, 1949–1950], (Moscow: AN SSSR, 1951):67.

30. A. A. Saburov, "Rabota Gor'kogo nad pervoi chast'iu romana *Zhizn' Klima Samgina* [Gorky's Work on the First Part of *The Life of Klim Samgin*]," in *Gor'kovskie chteniia*, 3 (1951): 113–16.

31. A discussion of the prototypes for Lyutov can be found in Ovcharenko, *Roman-epopeia M. Gor'kogo*, 113–14.

32. On some of the most likely models, see 25:52–57.

33. In the course of *The Life of Klim Samgin* Gorky mentions about a thousand literary works and heroes. See I. I. Vainberg, *Zhizn' Klima Samgina M. Gor'kogo: Istoriko-literaturnyi kommentarii* [Gorky's *The Life of*

Klim Samgin: A Historical and Literary Commentary] (Moscow: Prosveshchenie, 1971), 8.

34. At least some commentators seem to have been taken aback by the large number of religious motifs in the novel; see, e.g., I. S. Novich, *Khudozhestvennoe zaveshchanie Gor'kogo: Zhizn' Klima Samgina* [Gorky's Artistic Bequest: *The Life of Klim Samgin*] 2d ed., enl. (Moscow: Sovetskii pisatel', 1968), 472–75.

Chapter Seven

1. *G-30,* 24:483.
2. Ibid., 488.
3. Khodasevich, *Nekropol',* 254.
4. Lazar Fleishman, for instance, interprets Gorky's efforts during the turbulent 1930s as striving to create a better climate for literature. See his *Boris Pasternak v tridtsatye gody* [Boris Pasternak in the Thirties] (Jerusalem: The Magnes Press, Hebrew University, 1984), esp. chap. 6, 197–235, and chap. 9, 303–52).
5. B. V. Mikhailovskii, "Maksim Gor'kii," *Kratkaia literaturnaia entsiklopediia* [Concise Literary Encyclopedia], vol. 2 (Moscow: Sovetskaia entsiklopediia, 1964), cols. 285–96.
6. I. M. Bespalov, "Maksim Gor'kii," *Literaturnaia entsiklopediia* [Literary Encyclopedia], vol. 2 (Moscow: Izd. Kommunisticheskoi akademii, 1929), cols. 643–55; the quotation is from col. 654.

Selected Bibliography

PRIMARY SOURCES

1. In Russian

Gor'kii, M. *Polnoe sobranie sochinenii: Khudozhestvennye proizvedeniia v dvadtsati piati tomakh* [Complete Works: Artistic Writings in Twenty-Five Volumes]. Moscow: Nauka [Science], 1968–76; *Varianty* [Variants] [drafts of the above works]. 10 vols. Moscow: Nauka [Science], 1974–82.

————. *Sobranie sochinenii v tridtsati tomakh* [Collected Works in Thirty Volumes]. Moscow: GIKhL [Artistic Literature], 1949–56.

2. In English

Gorky, Maxim. *Collected Works in Ten Volumes.* Moscow: Progress, 1978–82. Includes a generous selection of the stories, six of the better-known plays, four novels *(Foma Gordeev, Mother, The Life of Matvei Kozhemiakin, The Artamonov Business)*, the autobiographical trilogy *(Childhood, In the World, My Universities)*, and selections of both essays and memoirs.

————. *Seven Plays.* Translated by Alexander Bakshy and Paul Nathan. New Haven: Yale University Press, 1945. Includes several of the lesser-known plays, including *Barbarians, Queer People (The Eccentrics)*, the first variant of *Vassa Zheleznova*, and *The Zykovs*.

————. *Best Short Stories.* Edited by Avrahm Yarmolinsky and Moura Budberg. New York: Grayson, 1947.

————. *The Confession.* Translated by Rose Strunsky. New York: Frederick A. Stokes Co., 1916.

————. *Creatures That Once Were Men.* Translated by J. K. M. Shirazi. New York: Funk & Wagnalls, 1906.

————. *Fragments from My Diary.* New York: McBride & Co., 1924.

————. *The Life of Klim Samgin.* 4 vols. *Bystander.* Translated by Bernard Guerney. New York: Literary Guild, 1930; *The Magnet.* Translated by Alexander Bakshy. New York: Jonathan Cape, 1931; *Other Fires.* Translated by Alexander Bakshy. New York: D. Appleton & Co., 1933; *The Specter.* Translated by Alexander Bakshy. New York: D. Appleton-Century, 1938.

————. *The Life of an Unnecessary Man.* Translated by Moura Budberg. New York: Doubleday, 1971.

————. *Reminiscences of Tolstoy, Chekhov, and Andreev.* Translated by S. S. Kosteliansky, Katherine Mansfield, and Leonard Woolf. London: Hogarth, 1934.

————. *Selected Short Stories.* Translated by B. Isaacs et al. New York: F. Ungar, 1959.

————. *Through Russia.* Translated by C. J. Hogarth. New York: E. P. Dutton, 1922.

————. *The Three of Them.* Translated by Alexandra Linden. London: T. F. Unwin, 1902.

————. *Unrequited Love and Other Stories.* Translated by Moura Budberg. New York: Ravin, 1949.

SECONDARY SOURCES

The following list includes most of the major studies devoted to Gorky in English but only a bare sampling of the books on Gorky in Russian. For further references, please see the notes.

Akademiia nauk SSSR [USSR Academy of Sciences]. *Arkhiv A. M. Gor'kogo* [The Gorky Archive]. 14 vols. Moscow: GIKhL [Artistic Literature] and Nauka, 1939–76. Several are devoted to correspondence between Gorky and some of the people close to him, including I. P. Ladyzhnikov, K. P. Pyatnitsky, Gorky's first wife, and his son.

————. *Gor'kovskie chteniia* [Readings on Gorky]. 10 vols. Moscow: AN SSSR [USSR Academy of Sciences] and Nauka, 1940–68. Many fine articles as well as notes pertaining to narrow questions concerning Gorky's life and works. Note that this same title has been used for some more recent collections of articles published in the city of Gorky.

————. *M. Gor'kii: Materialy i issledovaniia* [Gorky: Materials and Investigations]. 4 vols. Leningrad: AN SSSR [USSR Academy of Sciences], 1934–51. The four volumes contain a wealth of useful articles; many of the "materials" have been incorporated into the most recent edition of Gorky's works.

————. *Letopis' zhizni i tvorchestva A. M. Gor'kogo* [Chronology of Gorky's Life and Work]. 4 vols. Moscow: AN SSSR [USSR Academy of Sciences], 1958–60. A detailed listing of the events in Gorky's life; for the later years, provides almost a day-by-day account. While the volumes are occasionally reticent about matters that would be of interest, the wealth of factual information makes them a basic source for any biographical study.

Babaian, E. I. *Rannii Gor'kii: U ideinykh istokov tvorchestva* [The Early

Gorky: Ideological Sources of His Art]. Moscow: Khudozhestvennaia literatura [Artistic Literature], 1973. An original and sometimes provocative interpretation of the early stories.

Bialik, B. A. M. *Gor'kii—dramaturg* [Gorky as Playwright]. Moscow: Sovetskii pisatel' [Soviet Writer], 1962. Contains the most thorough treatment of the plays, though at times the sheer volume of information is overwhelming.

Borras, F. M. *Maxim Gorky the Writer: An Interpretation.* Oxford: Clarendon Press, 1967. A very solid study of Gorky's works; an attempt to define his "ideas and outlook" is followed by an examination of each genre in which he wrote.

Desnitskii, V. A. A. M. *Gor'kii: Ocherki zhizni i tvorchestva* [Gorky: Sketches of His Life and Work]. Moscow: GIKhL [Artistic Literature], 1959. This collection of articles includes several that deal with biographical matters and others on *Mother* and on Gorky's autobiographical trilogy. Desnitsky first met Gorky in Nizhny Novgorod before the turn of the century and in subsequent years did much to promote the study of his work.

Fedin, K. A. *Gor'kii sredi nas* [Gorky among Us], Moscow: Molodaia gvardiia [Young Guard], 1967. An account both of Gorky's relations with Fedin and more generally with the Serapion Brothers during the 1920s. Creates a sense of both Gorky's authority and of his efforts to help writers during the early Soviet years.

Golubeva, O. D. *Gor'kii—izdatel'* [Gorky as Publisher]. Moscow: Kniga [Book], 1968. Provides solid information regarding Gorky's various publishing ventures from the beginning of the century until his departure from the Soviet Union in 1921.

Gourfinkel, Nina. *Gorky.* New York: Grove Press, 1960. A generously illustrated biography that makes effective use of Gorky's own writings to depict the key moments in his life.

Gruzdev, I. A. *Gor'kii i ego vremia, 1868–1896* [Gorky and His Time, 1868–1896]. 3d ed., enl. Moscow: GIKhL [Artistic Literature], 1962. A very detailed account of Gorky's life and of the people who played a role in it by a person who knew Gorky well. This remains an authoritative source for Gorky's early years.

Hare, Richard. *Maxim Gorky: Romantic Realist and Conservative Revolutionary.* London: Oxford University Press, 1962. Deals primarily with Gorky's political development, emphasizing his differences with other Bolsheviks. Gorky's creative writing is discussed primarily to support remarks about his political outlook.

Holtzman, Filia. *The Young Maxim Gorky, 1868–1902.* New York: Columbia University Press, 1948. A well-documented study of his early career; uses the stories to trace developments in his outlook and includes an interesting chapter on his relationships with other writers.

Kastorskii, S. V. *Dramaturgiia M. Gor'kogo: Nabliudeniia nad ideino-khudozhestvennoi spetsifikoi* [Gorky's Plays: Observations on Their Specific
Ideological and Artistic Traits]. Moscow and Leningrad: Akademiia
nauk SSSR [USSR Academy of Sciences], 1963. More concise than
Bialik's study: some good observations on the main structural features
of individual plays.

Kaun, Alexander. *Maxim Gorky and His Russia.* New York: J. Cape and
H. Smith, [1931]. A lengthy biography that makes heavy use of
Gorky's autobiographical writings and stories. The work is in some
ways dated by now, but Kaun, who visited Gorky in Sorrento, provides a reliable and well-informed account that is still quite useful.

Khodasevich, V. F. "Gor'kii." In *Nekropol': Vospominaniia* [Necropolis:
Memoirs]. 1939. Reprint. Paris: YMCA-Press, 1976. The most extensive of several penetrating memoirs by Khodasevich on Gorky.
Page for page this remains the most insightful portrait of Gorky the
man.

Krutikova, N. E. *V nachale veka: Gor'kii i simvolisty* [A Century Begins:
Gorky and the Symbolists]. Kiev: Naukova dumka [Scientific
Thought], 1978. Tends to ignore or explain away any ambiguities
in Gorky's generally hostile attitude toward symbolism and Nietzsche.
Still, a very thorough study that explores many obscure sources.

Levin, Dan. *Stormy Petrel: The Life and Work of Maxim Gorky.* New York:
Appleton-Century, 1965. An idiosyncratic and factually not always
reliable account that nonetheless contains some interesting original
observations.

Literaturnoe nasledstvo [Literary Heritage]. 70 (1963), *Gor'kii i sovetskie
pisateli: Neizdannaia perepiska* [Gorky and Soviet Writers: Unpublished
Correspondence]. 72 (1965), *Gor'kii i Leonid Andreev: Neizdannaia
perepeiska* [Gorky and Leonid Andreev: Unpublished Correspondence].
74 (1965), *Iz tvorcheskogo naslediia sovetskikh pisatelei* [From the Creative
Legacy of Soviet Writers]. The first two of these volumes from a
valuable series of archival publications contain large collections of
letters; the latter has material on two of Gorky's plays and on *The
Life of Klim Samgin.*

Mikhailovskii, B. V., and Tager, E. B. *Tvorchestvo M. Gor'kogo* [Gorky's
Art]. 3d ed., rev. Moscow: Prosveshchenie [Enlightenment], 1969.
A good general introduction to Gorky's literary career by two scholars
who wrote on him extensively.

Muchnic, Helen. *From Gorky to Pasternak: Six Writers in Soviet Russia.* New
York: Random House, 1961. The essay on Gorky, while treating
only a few of his works in detail, nonetheless provides a sensitive
summary of his main strengths and weaknesses as a writer.

Nikitina, I. V. *Po sledam geroev Gor'kogo (Nizhegorodskii kommentarii k proizvedeniiam pisatelia)* [On the Trail of Gorky's Heroes (A Nizhny

Novgorod Commentary on the Writer's Works)]. Gorky: Volgo-
viatskoe knizhnoe izdatel'stvo [Volga-Vyatka Publishing House],
1981. Informed speculation on possible prototypes for Gorky's characters among the inhabitants of Nizhny Novgorod and, to a lesser
extent, other cities in the area. Also discusss the effect on Gorky's
works of his enforced stay in Arzamas.

Ovcharenko, A. I. M. *Gor'kii i literaturnye iskaniia XX stoletiia* [Gorky
and Literary Quests of the Twentieth Century]. Moscow: Sovetskii
pisatel' [Soviet Writer], 1971. This book, by a prolific writer on
Gorky, perhaps exaggerates his significance as an innovator, but it
does include good studies of Gorky's late works.

Segel, Harold B. *Twentieth-Century Russian Drama: From Gorky to the Present.*
New York: Columbia University Press, 1979. Includes the fullest
account in English of Gorky's career as a dramatist.

Volkov, A. A. *Put' khudozhnika: M. Gor'kii do Oktiabria* [The Artist's Way:
Gorky before the October Revolution]. Moscow: Khudozhestvennaia
literatura [Artistic Literature], 1969. Of Volkov's many studies devoted to Gorky, this offers the best analysis of Gorky's writing.
Includes many perceptive comments on Gorky's technique and on
the relationships among various works.

————. *A. M. Gor'kii i literaturnoe dvizhenie sovetskoi epokhi* [Gorky and
the Literary Movement of the Soviet Period]. 2d ed., enl. Moscow:
Sovetskii pisatel' [Soviet Writer], 1971. Describes Gorky's personal
connections with and literary influences on his fellow Soviet Writers,
especially during the 1920s.

Weil, Irwin. *Gorky: His Literary Development and Influence on Soviet Intellectual
Life.* New York: Random House, 1966. Offers a brief survey of
Gorky's career followed by a useful analysis of Gorky's role in Soviet
literature during the 1920s and afterwards.

Wolfe, Bertram. *The Bridge and the Abyss: The Troubled Friendship of Maxim
Gorky and V. I. Lenin.* New York: Praeger, 1967. Sheds light on an
important aspect of Gorky's biography; his differences with Lenin tell
much about Gorky's political beliefs.

Yale/Theatre. 7, no. 2 (1976). A special issue devoted to Gorky. Includes
a version of Segel's study and an English translation of Khodasevich's
memoir (see the above entries), along with other interesting items:
some on Gorky as playwright, but other on general aspects of Gorky's
writing and personality.

Zaburdaev, N. A. *V sem'e Kashirinykh* [The Kashirin Family]. Gorky:
Volgo-viatskoe knizhnoe izdatel'stvo [Volga-Vyatka Publishing
House], 1976. Complements Gruzdev's study by offering detailed
information on Gorky's family, particularly on his mother's side;
Zaburdaev's detective work has also uncovered a little more infor-
mation on Gorky's childhood.

Index